Historic Homes
of American Authors

Historic Homes of American Authors

IRVIN HAAS

THE PRESERVATION PRESS

The Preservation Press
National Trust for Historic Preservation
1785 Massachusetts Avenue, N.W.
Washington, D.C. 20036

The National Trust for Historic Preservation is the only private, non-profit organization chartered by Congress to encourage public participation in the preservation of sites, buildings, and objects significant in American history and culture. Support is provided by membership dues, endowment funds, contributions, and grants from federal agencies, including the U.S. Department of the Interior, under provisions of the National Historic Preservation Act of 1966. The opinions expressed here do not necessarily reflect the views or policies of the Interior Department. For information on membership, write to the Membership Office at the address above.

Printed in the United States of America
95 94 93 92 91   5 4 3 2 1

Library of Congress Cataloging in Publication Data
Haas, Irvin.
    Historic homes of American authors / Irvin Haas.
        p.   cm.
    Includes index.
    ISBN 0-89133-180-8
    1. Literary landmarks — United States — Guide-books. 2. Authors, American — Homes and haunts — Guide-books. 3. Architecture, Domestic — United States — Guide-books. 4. Historic buildings — United States — Guide-books. 5. Dwellings — United States — Guide-books. I. Title.
PS141.H28 1991
810.9 — dc20   90-23217

Designed and typeset by Meadows & Wiser, Washington, D.C.
Printed by McNaughton & Gunn, Saline, Michigan

Front cover: Line illustration of Washington Irving and Sunnyside, Irving's estate in Tarrytown, New York. (Courtesy of Historic Hudson Valley)
Back cover: Willa Cather and her girlhood home in Red Cloud, Nebraska. (Courtesy of Nebraska State Historical Society)
Opposite title page: Contemporary actors stroll in front of Irving's Sunnyside. (Courtesy of Historic Hudson Valley)

CONTENTS

8 PREFACE

10 CALIFORNIA

Glen Ellen ■ Jack London
Martinez ■ John Muir ■ Eugene O'Neill
Monterey ■ Robert Louis Stevenson

24 CONNECTICUT

Hartford ■ Harriet Beecher Stowe ■ Mark Twain
West Hartford ■ Noah Webster

36 FLORIDA

Cross Creek ■ Marjorie Kinnan Rawlings
Key West ■ Ernest Hemingway

45 GEORGIA

Atlanta ■ Joel Chandler Harris
Macon ■ Sidney Lanier

50 ILLINOIS

Galesburg ■ Carl Sandburg
Springfield ■ Vachel Lindsay

59 INDIANA

Greenfield ■ James Whitcomb Riley
Indianapolis ■ James Whitcomb Riley
Rome City ■ Gene Stratton-Porter

67 MAINE

Gardiner ■ Edwin Arlington Robinson
Portland ■ Henry Wadsworth Longfellow
South Berwick ■ Sarah Orne Jewett

78 MARYLAND
Baltimore ■ Edgar Allan Poe

81 MASSACHUSETTS
Amesbury ■ John Greenleaf Whittier
Amherst ■ Emily Dickinson
Boston ■ William Hickling Prescott
Cambridge ■ Henry Wadsworth Longfellow
Concord ■ Louisa May Alcott ■ Ralph Waldo
Emerson ■ Henry David Thoreau
Cummington ■ William Cullen Bryant
Lenox ■ Edith Wharton
Pittsfield ■ Herman Melville
Salem ■ Nathaniel Hawthorne

119 MICHIGAN
Niles ■ Ring Lardner

123 MINNESOTA
Sauk Centre ■ Sinclair Lewis

127 MISSISSIPPI
Oxford ■ William Faulkner

130 NEBRASKA
Red Cloud ■ Willa Cather

133 NEW HAMPSHIRE
Derry ■ Robert Frost
Portsmouth ■ Thomas Bailey Aldrich

141 NEW JERSEY
Camden ■ Walt Whitman

143 NEW YORK
Bronx ■ Edgar Allan Poe
Huntington ■ Walt Whitman

New York City ■ Theodore Roosevelt
North Hills ■ Christopher Morley
Oyster Bay ■ Theodore Roosevelt
Roslyn ■ William Cullen Bryant
Tarrytown ■ Washington Irving

163 NORTH CAROLINA
Asheville ■ Thomas Wolfe
Flat Rock ■ Carl Sandburg

171 OHIO
Columbus ■ James Thurber
Dayton ■ Paul Laurence Dunbar
Lucas ■ Louis Bromfield

183 PENNSYLVANIA
Philadelphia ■ Edgar Allan Poe

186 TEXAS
Austin ■ O. Henry
San Antonio ■ O. Henry

191 VIRGINIA
Richmond ■ Ellen Glasgow

195 WEST VIRGINIA
Hillsboro ■ Pearl S. Buck

197 WISCONSIN
West Salem ■ Hamlin Garland

200 PHOTOGRAPHIC SOURCES

202 AMERICAN AUTHORS AND THEIR HOMES

207 INDEX TO AUTHORS

208 ABOUT THE AUTHOR

PREFACE

"I hope they will leave some of the old places intact, for we need links with the past generations [and] there are few enough in America at best." — Reverend Samuel Longfellow

A house reflects its occupants. It emanates many of the foibles and favors of those whom it has sheltered. Of all those whom houses have protected, surely there could be a no more diverse or fascinating collection of occupants than writers. One of the most perceptive guides to the very essence of a writer's work is the author's home. Whether a residence of youth or middle age a home reveals the originality of the writer who lived there.

An author's home can help uncover the background, the taste, and the personality of its occupant. A tour of these historic and literary homes enables us to sense the very quintessence of the author's world. Readers will recognize the sources of locales and characters, because many authors used the rich fabric of their communities — the setting and environment surrounding it, the climate and the people in that town or city — in their writings.

When you visit these homes, you may enter a world you so well remember from a novel or short story. Or you may relive a particularly favorite passage as you recognize a special room or object used by an author. You will see where the author lived and worked. On the shelves are the books the author owned and read. The desk and chair both are inanimate witnesses to the creation of the books you admire. The author's bed, the art embellishing the walls, and the views from the windows contemplated each writing day — all of these played a vital role in the author's work, either directly or indirectly. You can sense the psychological impact these surroundings may have had on the writer.

This collection of homes of American authors will lead you

on a diverse literary journey. While including such well-known writers as Washington Irving and Eugene O'Neill, I have also selected several authors generally considered neither literary nor creative. Theodore Roosevelt, besides being one of our most colorful presidents, wrote a number of travel and adventure books that were bestsellers in his day. He was also an avid contributor to magazines on a variety of subjects. John Muir, the naturalist and explorer, was one of our first environmentalists. His books have become classics of outdoor literature. The books of Gene Stratton-Porter focus on nature rather than human passions. William H. Prescott is one of the greatest of American historians whose philosophical insight and lively style have placed his many works in the forefront of American historical writing. These writers deserve their place in the pantheon of American literature, and their homes deserve a place in this book as well.

This collection does not pretend to be a compendium of every home associated with all American authors. Some of these dwellings have been victims of the wrecker's ball — the bitter price we must pay for urban "advancement." Others are now the private residences of individuals who want to preserve their privacy, although a few privately owned sites are included. Most of these owners are amenable to occasional visits if permission is sought in advance. Perhaps, in the final analysis, my own personal likes and dislikes have played some part in the sites I have chosen.

A state-by-state tour of the historic homes of American authors in these pages will stimulate and enhance your visits to the actual sites. Days and hours the properties are open have been included but are subject to change. Plan to contact a property before visiting to confirm visiting hours and admission fees, if any. The list of homes at the back of the book, arranged alphabetically by author, gives the name, address, and phone number, if available, for each of the properties included.

—— Glen Ellen ——

■

JACK LONDON

Born in San Francisco in 1876, Jack London fought his way up out of the factories and waterfront dives of West Oakland, California, to become the highest paid, most popular novelist and short-story writer of his day. At 17 he shipped out as an able seaman to the Japan and Bering seas. He sought gold in the Klondike, followed the Russo-Japanese War as a newspaper correspondent, and in 1914 was a war correspondent in Mexico. He wove his first-

Jack and Charmian London with friends Martin and Osa Johnson and an unidentified associate on the porch of the London ranch cottage.

hand experiences into stories of high adventure, which continue to appeal to millions of people around the world.

Famed for his exploits, he was a celebrity and a colorful and controversial personality. Generally good natured and playful, he could be combative and quick to side with the underdog. He was an eloquent speaker and much sought after as a lecturer on socialism and other economic and political topics. Despite his avowed socialism, most considered him a living symbol of rugged individualism and one of the most attractive and romantic figures of his time.

The Sonoma Valley's magnificent natural landscape, a unique combination of high hills, fields, and streams and a beautiful forest, appealed especially to London, whose work was passionate about the great questions of life and death and the struggle to survive with dignity and integrity. London first settled here in 1905 with his wife Charmian on a farm of "130

The ranch cottage, now being restored. Charmian London is sitting on the steps.

Wolf House, close to completion in 1913 and in ruins with
the Valley of the Moon in the distance, a vista especially valued
by London. Trees now obscure this view.

acres of the most beautiful, primitive land to be found in California." By this time he had become well known for his book *The Call of the Wild,* published in 1903 and still one of the greatest dog stories ever written.

He cared little that the farm was badly run-down. All he wanted was a "quiet place to write and loaf in." Soon, however, he was busy buying farm equipment and livestock for his "mountain ranch." He began work on a new barn and started to plan a fine new house, to be called Wolf House.

Not satisfied with the challenges presented by the ranch, London built a ship, the *Snark,* and set sail with Charmian for a seven-year voyage around the world. The journey lasted only 27 months. Beset by health problems, London sold the *Snark* and returned to Glen Ellen.

Over the next three years, beginning in 1909, he bought more land and in 1911 moved to a cottage in the middle of his holdings. Work on London's dream house—a grand house built to last 1,000 years—began in earnest. The house was complete in August 1913 and plans were made to move London's specially designed furniture into the mansion. In the early morning hours of August 22, word came that the house was burning. By the time London reached the site, nothing could be done to save it. The house's walls stand today, a reminder of London's and Charmian's great dream. The entire house had stood on an extra-thick, earthquake-proof concrete slab.

The fire, whose suspicious origins are still a mystery, was a crushing financial blow to London, and the house's destruction left him severely depressed. He forced himself to go back to work, adding a new study to the little wood-frame cottage. He continued to write and travel, but his greatest satisfaction came from his ranch activities and his ambitious plans for expanding and increasing its productivity. These plans kept him perpetually in debt and under intense pressure to keep writing to pay for his beloved ranch projects. His doctors urged him to ease up, to change his working habits and his diet, to stop all use of alcohol. His refusal to change his lifestyle or pace led in 1916 to his early death at age 40 of uremia.

As a testament to London, his widow built the House of Happy Walls between 1919 and 1922. Situated on a knoll surrounded by a mixed oak, bay, and madrone forest, it has the same Spanish-style roof and walls of volcanic stone of Wolf House but is smaller and more formal. After her death in 1955, Charmian London directed that this house be used as a memorial to London. Today it serves as a museum and visitor center to the Jack London State Historic Park, encompassing the Jack London Ranch, the remains of Wolf House, and the 1860s cottage where London worked from 1911 to 1916. The cottage, being restored to its 1916 appearance, is not open to the public but can easily be viewed from the outside, including the front porches enclosed by London for sleeping. In addition, a stone structure, once part of a winery next to the cottage, had been used by the Londons as a living area and kitchen.

The Jack London State Historic Park is administered by California's Department of Parks and Recreation. Hours begin at 8 a.m. to the closing time posted at the entrance station. The House of Happy Walls museum is open daily, 10 a.m. to 5 p.m., except Thanksgiving, Christmas, and New Year's Day.

──────────────── Martinez ────────────────

■

JOHN MUIR

John of the Mountains they called him. He lived and earned the title. Intimately linked, John Muir's life and writing championed American wilderness at a crucial point in history. He moved us to preserve exquisite examples of our natural heritage before it was too late, before the last remnants were gobbled up by the relentless wheels of industry.

House where Muir and his family lived in the Alhambra Valley.

John Muir, fourth from right, standing next to Theodore Roosevelt in Mariposa Grove, Yosemite.

Born in 1838 near Dunbar, Scotland, Muir once wrote, "As a boy I was fond of everything that was wild, and all my life I've been growing fonder and fonder of wild places and wild creatures." In 1848, when he was 10, Muir immigrated with his family to the Wisconsin frontier. His father, a preacher and farmer, and John turned their energies to clearing trees, planting crops, and building—to tame the American wilderness that he would later struggle to preserve. After attending the University of Wisconsin, Muir eventually sought the "university of the wilderness," a lifelong course of study. He set out on foot, crossing the country from north to south, and ended up finally in the High Sierras of California—ever after the center of his quest for wild nature's meaning.

California became his home and its mountains the dwelling place of his spirit, the setting for his influential writings. Ralph Waldo Emerson, Henry David Thoreau, and John Burroughs had also written of wild nature, but they had not lived in it as

Muir did. Muir's writings have the force of his personal experience and perceptive observations.

In 1880 he married Louie Wanda Strentzel and for the first time in 29 years settled down to a domestic life that included running his father-in-law's fruit ranch in the Alhambra Valley of California. He earned the family a modest fortune in this decade, and the couple had two daughters to whom Muir was devoted. But this type of success was not personally satisfying to Muir, and, at the encouragement of his wife, he resumed his wilderness travels and studies in areas scattered around the globe from Alaska to Africa, concentrating in the nearby Sierras. His observations and writings made valuable contributions to scientific knowledge in the field of glaciology, and he personally discovered several glaciers, including one in Alaska that bears his name.

Muir spoke out for saving wilderness just when the frontier that molded our pioneer character was disappearing. The important change in national attitude that Muir's campaign represented in the late 1800s is difficult to appreciate today. We now recognize our culture's close link to our environment's fate—thanks in large part to John Muir. He bridged the gap between earlier exploitive attitudes toward wildlands and today's environmental outlook.

In addition to writing extensively about preserving the wilderness for magazines and newspapers, Muir was one of the founders of the Sierra Club in 1892 and served as its president until his death in 1914. His first book was published in 1894 and many of his works are reprinted today.

Administered by the National Park Service of the U.S. Department of the Interior, the 8.8-acre John Muir National Historic Site preserves the house of John Muir as well as a small part of the fruit ranch where he lived from 1890 until his death. The house is an Italianate structure built in 1882 by Muir's father-in-law. The house and grounds are open daily from 10 a.m. to 4:30 p.m., except on Thanksgiving, Christmas, and New Year's Day.

■

EUGENE O'NEILL
Tao House

U ntil he came to Tao House, Eugene O'Neill had been a wanderer. Born in New York City on October 16, 1888, to actors James O'Neill and Ella Quinlan O'Neill, Eugene spent his infancy in hotel rooms and theater wings. As he grew older he was sent to Catholic schools and to Princeton University. In 1909 he sailed to Honduras on a gold-prospecting expedition, later traveling to South America in 1910 and to West Africa on a tramp steamer in 1911. He drank a great deal, lived for a time in a waterfront flophouse in Manhattan, attempted suicide, and, when he was 24, fell ill with tuberculosis. In the sanitarium, he was forced to pause for the first time.

His illness arrested, he began to write. In summer 1916 in Provincetown, Massachusetts, he fell in with a group of amateur actors who staged his short play, *Bound East for Cardiff*, with such success that his ambition to write plays was affirmed. Critical and popular successes followed. In 1920 he received the first of four Pulitzer Prizes.

By the time he came to California in 1936, 35 of his plays had been produced. Working on several plays at the same time, he always needed absolute isolation to ensure continuous and undisturbed concentration. This same year he was awarded the Nobel Prize for Literature, and with this cash prize he determined to build the home he came to call his "final harbor," Tao House.

Shut away by Tao House's thick walls and the three doors leading to his study, O'Neill came at last to the work-centered world he had sought for so long. From his study, as he wrote, he could look out on Mount Diablo and the fertile floor of the San Ramon Valley. He began to write a series of autobiographical plays in which he explored his own past.

Eugene O'Neill and Tao House, O'Neill's "final harbor."

O'Neill and his wife Carlotta were to live in Tao House less than a decade, between 1937 and 1944. He became ill with Parkinson's disease, and tremors made it impossible to write. World War II cut off the life-support systems of the house; servants were unavailable; and transportation impossible. Inevitably, O'Neill left his sanctuary. Effectively silenced by illness, he died in a Boston hotel in 1953.

The name of Tao House comes from the ancient Chinese philosophical system ascribed to the sage Lao-Tze, who placed a high value on mystical contemplation as a way of finding the truth. Tao means the right path, the "way" to righteous knowledge. While O'Neill was not a Taoist, his life was devoted to an intense search for inner truth, and he often wrote in words similar to those of the teachers of Taoism.

O'Neill discovered the site for Tao House during a sightseeing trip through the San Francisco Bay area. When he and his wife came to the Las Trampas hills, they felt they had come

Front of the Stevenson House, once known as the French Hotel.

home. Major planning for the house was handled by Carlotta O'Neill, and the design and style—California Mission with touches of the Orient—reflect her taste. The block walls simulate an adobe structure, while black tiles carry out an Oriental motif. The O'Neills wanted a dark and quiet house with few carpets and no drapery. The blue ceilings and dark floors of tile or black-stained planks contrasted with the Chinese red doors and white walls. In the living room, entry hall, and master bedroom, dark mirrors reflected the light; living in the house must have seemed like living in the shadowy recesses of an elegant cave. Every room, however, opened directly out of doors.

Visits to Tao House, administered by the National Park Service of the U.S. Department of the Interior, are by reservation only. Public tours are offered Wednesday through Sunday, except Christmas, Thanksgiving, and New Year's Day.

--------------------------- Monterey ---------------------------

■

ROBERT LOUIS STEVENSON

While Robert Louis Stevenson is not considered an American writer, his experiences in the United States influenced him and his writing significantly, including, during his first stay, a difficult cross-country journey and a trip into wilderness that almost resulted in his death. He was in the United States for two separate parts of his life: between 1879 and 1880, primarily in California, and between 1887 and 1889 in New York.

Born in Edinburgh, Scotland, in 1850, Stevenson was handicapped by ill health from early youth. After formal schooling, he studied engineering at Edinburgh University, changed to law, and was called to the bar in 1875, but he never practiced. For health reasons he began to travel extensively and gradually devoted himself to writing exclusively.

While traveling in France on holiday, he met Fanny Osbourne, an American studying art in that country. He followed
her to California and a few months later, after Osbourne's divorce became final, they were married. They spent their hon-
eymoon in the Napa Valley near St. Helena, California, where
Stevenson wrote *The Silverado Squatters*. He recorded his trip

Robert Louis Stevenson

to America in *The Amateur Emigrant* and *Across the Plain.*

Stevenson returned to Scotland in 1880 but returned to the United States after he had become established as a popular writer in 1887, this time to write essays for *Scribner's Magazine* and to begin *The Master of Ballantrae.* He also sought to improve his health at Saranac Lake, New York.

At the time he was in Monterey, Stevenson was poor, unknown, and in frail health. He occupied a second-floor room in a boarding house known as the French Hotel, since renamed the Stevenson House. The author described his accommodations there as a "bright sunny room on the West side of the house." A two-story adobe, the original portion of the building, dates from the late 1830s when it was the home of Rafael Gonzales, first administrator of customs for Alta, California. In 1856 Juan Girardin and his wife, Manuela Perez, bought the house. They made additions and rented spare bedrooms, sheltering many of the artists and writers of the Monterey Peninsula, such as Stevenson.

Stevenson House is typical of the other adobe structures that make up the scattered sites of the Monterey State Historic Park, located in downtown Monterey and administered by California's Department of Parks and Recreation. Adobes were made with sun-dried clay bricks; walls are typically 36 to 40 inches thick; and many have redwood plank floors. The additions to the Stevenson House are made of lumber, for the most part.

Neglected over the years, the house was slated to be torn down in 1940. Stevenson fans bought the building and gave it to the state as a museum. The author's stepdaughter donated many of the furnishings and memorabilia. The ground floor is devoted to Robert Louis Stevenson with the exception of a Mexican *sala*, or living room. The second floor is furnished with period pieces representing the living quarters of the Girardin family. The room Stevenson occupied as a boarder displays a velvet jacket that was his.

The Stevenson House is shown by guided tour only and is closed on Wednesdays.

──────────────── Hartford ────────────────

■

HARRIET BEECHER STOWE

Although Harriet Beecher Stowe wrote a number of books, she is best known for *Uncle Tom's Cabin,* a novel embodying her deeply felt horror of slavery. Born in 1811 in Litchfield, Connecticut, to a minister's family, she developed an early interest in theology and schemes for bettering humanity. In 1832 her father became president of Lane Seminary School in Cincinnati, and she taught school there until she married Calvin Ellis Stowe in 1836. She wrote stories to add to her husband's meager income as a teacher. In 1850 her husband was appointed to a professorship at Bowdoin College, and it was in Brunswick, Maine, that Stowe penned her classic work.

Uncle Tom's Cabin, partly inspired by Stowe's meeting with an African American preacher, Josiah Henson, was translated into many foreign languages. While visiting Europe in 1853, she was overwhelmed with honors, but, in spite of the book's popularity, the author was always beset with financial worries. Six children added to the financial burden. To support her family, she wrote more than 30 novels, as well as biographies, poetry, nonfiction, and children's stories.

Harriet Beecher Stowe had known the Nook Farm area of Hartford long before it was settled. From 1826 to 1832 she had been a student and then a teacher at the Hartford Female Seminary, founded by her sister Catherine Beecher. She promised herself that one day she would build a dream house at Nook

Stowe's study in the house on Forest Street. The oval paintings above the desk were inspired by the author's well-known work.

Harriet Beecher Stowe

Harriet Beecher Stowe House, reflecting the cottage architecture popular during the first half of the 19th century.

Farm, then on the western edge of the city. Finally, in 1864 she built Oakholm, an eight-gabled Gothic Revival villa. When the house became too burdensome to maintain, she sold it and settled into this more modest cottage on Forest Street in 1873, also part of Nook Farm, which by then was inhabited by a number of literary figures and social reformers, including Mark Twain and William Gillette, the noted actor and play-wright.

Built in 1871, the Forest Street house reflects the 19th-century cottage architecture popularized by the architects and landscape designers Andrew Jackson Downing and Calvert

Vaux. The house's facade belies its size, giving the impression the house is smaller and more cottage-like than it is. Two bay windows, varied porches on each side, and graceful exterior wood trim combined with a steep hip roof contribute to the house's pleasing sense of proportion. Gardens, modeled after those maintained by Stowe during her residency from 1873 until her death in 1896, surround the cottage.

Inside, the cottage boasts a typical and eclectic Victorian taste for collecting. Heirlooms from the 18th century are juxtaposed to Second Empire and High Victorian pieces. Paint-

Mark Twain and family on the porch, or *ombra,* of their Hartford house, left to right, Clara, Livy, Jean, Samuel, and Susy Clemens.

ings purchased on Stowe's European tours are next to her own competent oils and watercolors. Photographs and portraits of family members are found in many rooms. Throughout, souvenirs of her travels and favorite bric-a-brac abound.

Stowe's love of nature is emphasized inside through the use of plants in place of curtains or draperies on the bay windows. In the dining room stand her table and a set of period chairs. On the Victorian sideboard, decorated with bird and fruit carvings, are pieces of silver. Through the bay window of her bedroom, Stowe could enjoy a view of her garden and Mark Twain's home beyond. She did much of her writing in the sitting room next to her bedroom. She herself decorated the bureau, bedside stand, and cane-seated chair. The kitchen is modeled after a design in *The American Woman's Home,* written by Stowe and her sister to suggest new and modern ways to make the home more efficient, clean, and sanitary.

The Stowe-Day Foundation complex on Farmington Avenue consists of a visitor center, the Harriet Beecher Stowe House, the Katherine S. Day House, a library, and the Mark Twain House. The Stowe House is open Tuesday to Saturday, 9:30 a.m. to 4 p.m., Sundays, noon to 4 p.m., and, between June 1 and Columbus Day and all of December, on Mondays, 9:30 a.m. to 4 p.m.

■

MARK TWAIN

Mark Twain's first impression of Hartford was overwhelmingly positive. "Of all the beautiful towns it has been my fortune to see, this is the chief. . . . You do not know what beauty is if you have not been here." In 1870 he had married Olivia Longdon, an American he had met on his European sojourn, and the couple had decided to settle in Hartford. Twain bought land in a western area of the city known as Nook Farm and engaged Edward

Gothic Revival house of the Clemens family.

Tuckerman Potter, a New York City architect, to design a house. The family moved into their completed home in October 1874. Here, Twain entered the most productive phase of his literary career. Before the family left in 1891, Twain had written seven major works including *Tom Sawyer* and *Huckleberry Finn*.

Born Samuel Langhorne Clemens in Florida in 1835, Twain had spent his childhood in Hannibal, Missouri, amid surroundings he was later to immortalize in his stories. His famous pseudonym, Mark Twain, was derived from the call of the leadsman on riverboats when a depth of two fathoms was sounded.

After the death of his father in 1847, Twain worked for his brother, Orion, on the *Hannibal Journal* for a few years and then made his way to the cities of the East and Midwest, where he worked as a printer. In 1857, while on a trip to New Orleans, he decided to become a riverboat pilot. After two years he moved from the river west to Carson City, Nevada, to join his brother. When some of his get-rich-quick schemes failed, he began reporting for the *Virginia City* (Nev.) *Enterprise* under the name Mark Twain.

His first fame as a writer came with the publication of "Jim Smiley and the Jumping Frog" in the *New York Saturday Press* in 1865. Later, on his return from the Sandwich Islands, where he had been sent by the *Sacramento* (Calif.) *Union*, he became a successful humorous lecturer. His first book, *The Celebrated Jumping Frog of Calaveras County*, was published in 1867. That same year he visited the Holy Land, and in 1869 he published his second book, the very popular *Innocents Abroad*, an account of his journey.

The house that Twain and his wife "Livy" built was a High Victorian Gothic Revival mansion, characterized by steeply pitched roofs and an asymmetrical layout of bay windows, gables, and turrets. The rich exterior brickwork was enlivened by a bold use of black and vermilion paint. A long veranda, the *ombra,* and a large south porch on the third floor called the "Texas deck" have contributed to the myth that the house was designed to look like a riverboat. The kitchen wing was enlarged in 1881 and major rooms redecorated on the first floor with the guidance of Associated Artists, a New York firm that included Louis Comfort Tiffany.

Bad business investments and the high cost of maintaining their lifestyle forced the family to leave Hartford in 1891. Plans to return to the house were abandoned when Susy, the eldest daughter, died there in 1896 of spinal meningitis during a visit to Hartford. Memories of their beloved child and their happiest periods together were so tied to the house that the family did not sell until 1903.

In 1929 the Friends of Hartford raised money to purchase the building as a memorial to Mark Twain. The downstairs guest room became the memorial's headquarters. Upstairs apartments were rented for income, and a branch office of the Hartford Public Library occupied the rest of the first floor. Finally in 1955, restoration began to return the house to the period of Twain's occupancy. It had been a 25-year commitment; in 1974, the centennial of the house, it became a house museum and a living memorial to the author.

The Mark Twain House is open all year except Thanksgiving, December 24 and Christmas, New Year's Day, Easter, and Labor Day. Between June 1 and August 31, hours are daily, 10 a.m. to 4:30 p.m.; between September 1 and May 31, hours are Tuesday to Saturday, 9:30 a.m. to 4 p.m., and Sunday, 1 to 4 p.m.

Noah Webster House, a familiar saltbox design popular in New England.

■

NOAH WEBSTER

I
n the course of his 85 years, Noah Webster worked as a
schoolteacher, lawyer, editor, legislator, lecturer, and writer.
He wrote extensively on many subjects, including farming,
economics, disease, linguistics, science, religion, and, with
passionate intensity, on the importance of national unity
and the concept of a stronger federal system. He was one of the
founders of Amherst College, and he fathered some of the first
American copyright laws.

One of five children, he was born in 1758 when West Hartford was still part of Hartford. His father was a weaver and
farmer who worked his land with the aid of his sons. Webster
left his father's farm at the age of 16 to attend Yale University.
He graduated with the class of 1778 into an economy left
sorely depressed by the Revolutionary War and under an in-
ept government trying vainly to function with the limited and
crippling powers granted under the Articles of Confedera-
tion—an effort that he derided as a "ridiculous farce, a bur-
lesque on government, a reproach to America."

Webster produced and published in 1783 the first truly
American speller and guide to pronunciation. He borrowed
freely from the existing British prototypes but gave his speller
a distinctly American thrust. His book, which subsequently
underwent innumerable editions and revisions, would in time
sell close to 100 million copies. When he was 67, Webster first
published the classic *An American Dictionary of the English
Language*, the first of five editions he was to publish. In his 70s
his work included several new textbooks, a widely used *History of the United States*, and a translation of the Bible.

The Noah Webster House is not only the birthplace and
boyhood home of the author and lexicographer, but a fine example of early 18th-century American architecture. Like so

many of its contemporaries, the four-room house was erected around a massive central chimney. The cavernous fireplace, a source of heat and light, dominates the kitchen. The lean-to, which gives the house its familiar saltbox appearance, was added at the end of the 18th century. Directly across from the front door and abutting the massive chimney, a steep, narrow

Renowned lexicographer Noah Webster.

staircase ascends from the porch to the sleeping quarters above. The large room to the left of the porch was a combination living-dining-cooking room, dominated by its expansive fireplace. Noteworthy in this oldest section of the house are the corner cupboard; encased summer beams, with their original molding; exposed floor joists and the unusually large fireplace stretching across a major part of the kitchen's chimney wall. Two brick "beehive" ovens are recessed into the back wall of the fireplace, and the chimney wall is paneled with wide pine boards, simply molded and unpainted.

As the family expanded, a second stage of construction led to the addition of an upstairs parlor and parlor chamber, both on the opposite side of the chimney. In this way a structure was created of four rooms, two upstairs and two down. This arrangement was representative of typical Connecticut floor plans of the period.

The house was restored in 1967, and the period furnishings have been carefully selected to re-create the charm and authenticity of this home where Noah Webster spent his early life.

The Noah Webster House, administered by the Noah Webster Foundation and Historical Society of West Hartford, is open between June 15 and September 30, Monday, Tuesday, Thursday and Friday, 10 a.m. to 4 p.m., and weekends, 1 to 4 p.m. It is also open 1 to 4 p.m. each day but Wednesday between October 1 and June 14.

——————————— Cross Creek ———————————

■

MARJORIE KINNAN RAWLINGS

Until Marjorie Kinnan Rawlings, a journalist by trade, moved to Cross Creek in 1928, she had struggled without success to express her creativity. It was here in north-central Florida's scrub country that the land and its people touched something in the 32-year-old Rawlings; she began producing works that earned her a reputation as a talented writer, eventually winning the Pulitzer Prize for fiction in 1939 for her most famous work, *The Yearling,* the story of a boy's coming-of-age.

The people of Cross Creek, black and white, formed the grist for Rawlings's literary mill. She saw neighbors whose everyday lives were filled with interesting facets and ways of dealing with situations that threatened to overwhelm them — and sometimes did. She committed herself to Cross Creek and its inhabitants, writing five other novels, *Jacob's Ladder, Golden Apples, South Moon Under, When the Whippoorwill,* and *The Secret River.* Her last book, *The Sojourner,* was the only one to use a northern setting.

The house where Rawlings lived appears much as it does today; it is a modest frame dwelling with a low-hung gable roof, built some time before the mid-1890s. Rawlings added indoor plumbing and a carport and widened and screened-in the front porch. Houses such as this are well adapted to the local climate. Open porches and many windows allow cross-ventilation, while the kitchen — and sometimes the dining area — are sited away from the main living and sleeping areas so inhabitants will not

Marjorie Kinnan Rawlings in one of her citrus groves.

suffer the heat generated from cooking and baking with a wood-fired stove during the hot summers of central Florida.

Staying warm in winter was as much a challenge as keeping cool in summer. While winter usually was a matter of only a few cool months, these could be punctuated by spells of severe cold. Central heat was almost unknown in this area until World War II, and most residents used wood in fireplaces or small stoves to keep warm. Majorie Rawlings did the same.

She furnished her home in a practical and comfortable manner. The front porch contained several deerhide chairs and a

Rawlings's bungalow in Florida.

large table made partly from a cabbage palm log. There she did much of her writing. She was somewhat more conventional in furnishing other areas of the house.

Majorie Rawlings did not buy the Cross Creek house seeking solitude and a place to hide from the world. Along with the house came a farm, which Rawlings worked. Across from the house, you can stroll down the Grove Trail to visit one of her projects, a former orange and grapefruit grove, once a pecan grove. It was probably better suited to raising pecans. Since the 1950s almost all the citrus trees have succumbed to frost. The area to the south of the house was also planted in citrus, with a barn near the roadside and a tenant house further south. The house's grounds include a kitchen garden on the west side. All of these areas are important to the author's fiction, as they formed the stage on which her friends and neighbors acted out their lives.

In 1941 Rawlings married Norton Baskin and then divided her time between their home in St. Augustine and the retreat at Cross Creek until her death in 1953.

The Rawlings State Historic Site is administered by Florida's Department of Natural Resources, Division of Recreation and Parks. The house is open daily, except Tuesday and Wednesday, 10 to 11:30 a.m. and 1 to 4:30 p.m., with tours on the half hour.

Key West

■

ERNEST HEMINGWAY

Born in Oak Park, Illinois, in 1899, Ernest Hemingway led a colorful existence. His upbringing was upper middle class; his father was a medical doctor and his mother had trained as a singer. He was a good student and always a lover of the wild outdoors. When he graduated from high school, he skipped college and, with the help

Ernest Hemingway with a catch.

of an uncle, got a job as a reporter with the *Kansas City Star.*

During World War I he enlisted to drive ambulances for the Red Cross in 1918, volunteering to serve the front-line trenches. On duty he became one of the first Americans wounded on the Italian front, and newspapers reported his heroism in carrying another man to safety even with dozens of pieces of shrapnel in his own legs. After recovering from his wounds in Milan, Italy, he returned to Illinois, married Hadley Richardson in 1919, and went to live and work in Paris with his new wife. Their marriage fell apart in 1926.

In 1928 Hemingway first came to Key West with his second wife, Pauline Pfeiffer, an American heiress. It was in Key West that Hemingway wrote many of best-known works. He began with *A Farewell to Arms,* finishing it in spring 1929 to the accolades of his old friends, Scribner's editor Max Perkins and novelist John Dos Passos, who both proclaimed it magnificent. Hemingway and his wife made a number of trips abroad but kept returning to Key West. In 1931 the author finally purchased a dilapidated coralstone mansion that was to serve as home for the family, including two sons, Gregory and Patrick, for the next 15 years.

During World War II, Hemingway spent most of his time in Cuba and Key West. He worked semi-officially through the United States Embassy in Cuba patrolling the seas in his boat *Pilar* searching for German submarines. As a journalist, he covered D-Day and the final Allied push to victory in Europe. This period also saw his third marriage — to Martha Gellhorn.

He married his fourth wife, Mary, in 1946, and they settled in Cuba for more than 10 years. In 1959 the Hemingways left Cuba, where the political situation was unstable, for Ketchum, Idaho, where they purchased a house a few miles from the resort of Sun Valley. At this stage, the author was not well. Besides having high blood pressure, he was treated for depression, and several incidents seemed to indicate suicidal tendencies. Then, in Ketchum in 1961, he took his own life with

Studio where Hemingway wrote *A Farewell to Arms*.

a shotgun in the little entry hall room where he liked to work. He was buried in a small cemetery in Ketchum.

The house in Key West is a Spanish Colonial style and was built in 1851 by Asa Tift, a wealthy shipping magnate, using coral quarried right at the site, the quarry hole becoming the house's basement. Floor-to-ceiling windows function as doors leading to porches that encircle the structure on both levels. The Hemingways refurbished the home with European antiques and oil paintings, animal trophies, and artifacts from their worldwide trips. The property was landscaped, and a wall was built to discourage sightseers attracted by Hemingway's increasing fame. Plants from all over the world were added to augment the trees and plants already there.

The family renovated the large outbuilding behind the main

Hemingway's house, a side view.

house, once a carriage house and servants' quarters, and, in a quiet upper room, Hemingway made a workplace to write his books. Among the books written there were *Death in the Afternoon, Green Hills of Africa, To Have and Have Not,* and *For Whom the Bell Tolls.* One of the mansion's upstairs rooms is filled with memorabilia of Hemingway's life. Ornately carved Oriental cabinets hold old photographs dating back to his days of ambulance work. The dining room is lighted by an ornate chandelier of handblown Venetian glass. The spacious living room serves as a welcome center for today's guests. Descendants of Hemingway's six-toed cats still roam the grounds and are well-treated felines.

The Ernest Hemingway Home and Museum, a National Historic Landmark, is open daily, 9 a.m. to 5 p.m.

GEORGIA

———————————————— Atlanta ————————————————

■

JOEL CHANDLER HARRIS
The Wren's Nest

Joel Chandler Harris, who recorded the Uncle Remus stories, was born in 1848 in Eatonton, Georgia, the illegitimate son of a central Georgia seamstress and an Irish day laborer. He began his career in journalism at an early age, serving as a "printer's devil" in 1862 for a plantation newspaper published near his hometown. That career would carry him from the fields of Putnam County to Macon and Forsyth, Georgia, and to New Orleans before he settled in Atlanta and began to make a name for himself as a writer.

Harris accepted a job with the *Atlanta Constitution* in 1876, writing editorials by day and tales of Br'er Rabbit, Br'er Bear, and Br'er Fox by night. The stories of Uncle Remus, first published in the Atlanta newspaper, were syndicated throughout the country and also appeared in magazines and in book form. The first book, published in November 1880 as *Uncle Remus: His Songs and Sayings,* established Harris's national reputation as a storyteller and chronicler of the African American experience in the Old South. Eventually his works were translated into 27 languages. During his life Harris wrote some 33 books, six of them collections of Uncle Remus tales.

Harris remained in Atlanta working with the newspaper for 25 years, despite offers to leave from the *Washington Post* and *Century* magazine. He officially retired in 1900 but continued to write editorials until 1907, when he became editor of a new magazine, *Uncle Remus' Home Magazine,* at the urging of his

Joel Chandler Harris on the front porch of the Wren's Nest, c. 1906.

son Julian. He died in 1908, having recently converted to Roman Catholicism. He was buried in Atlanta's historic Westview Cemetery.

When the Harris family first moved into the Wren's Nest in 1881, the house looked much different than it does today. It was laid out in a "dogtrot" pattern—a central hallway flanked by rooms on either side and front and back doors opposite each other—a common type throughout the South. In this case, the Harris family of three adults and five children moved into a house of five rooms with a kitchen in the basement. A simple porch was decorated with modest Victorian ornamentation. In 1884 Harris began the house's dramatic transformation to the Queen Anne–Eastlake style we see today. He hired an architect to add a large porch to the house's facade and to build six new spaces, created by elongating the hallway and building rooms on either side of the new hallway addition. A final addition was made in 1900 when a bathroom was added. The family also installed electricity, indoor plumbing, and a central coal furnace.

Administered by the Joel Chandler Harris Association, Wren's Nest is open Tuesday to Saturday, 10 a.m. to 5 p.m., and Sunday, 2 to 5 p.m. It is closed on major holidays.

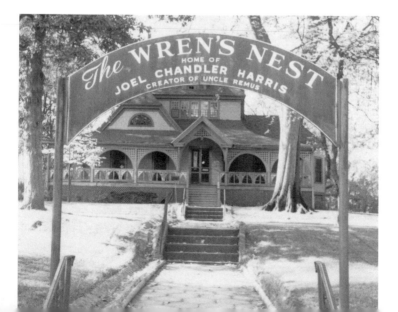

■

SIDNEY LANIER

This southern poet was a man of great versatility. He received recognition as a linguist, mathematician, lawyer, soldier, teacher, and musician. Of the many musical instruments he played well, he received special acclaim for his flute playing. He studied law, passed the bar, and practiced for a few years with his father and uncle in Macon. But music and poetry were Lanier's life expression. Among his best-known poems are "The Song of the Chattahoochee," "The Marshes of Glynn," "The Crystal," "Trees and the Master," "The Symphony," and "Sunrise."

Lanier was born in 1842 in this quaint Victorian cottage on High Street. At his birth, his father, Robert Samson Lanier, whose Huguenot forebears had settled in Virginia in 1716, was just starting his law practice in the little town of Griffin, Georgia, 60 miles north of Macon. The family moved to Griffin shortly after Lanier's birth, but the poet's ties to Macon remained strong throughout his life. He completed his elementary schooling there. An uncle on his mother's side was a prominent Macon lawyer who later was a member of the Confederate Congress and at one time attorney general of Georgia.

When the family returned some years later to Macon, they lived for a while at the Lanier Hotel, operated by Lanier's father and grandfather in the 1850s. It was the center of political and social activities, including a stopover by Confederate President Jefferson Davis, en route to prison after capture by Union soldiers at Irwinville, Georgia, in 1865.

The poet attended Old Oglethorpe College near Milledgeville, Georgia, graduating with first honors, and taught there until entering the Confederate Army with the Macon Volunteers in 1861 when he was 19. During the Civil War, Lanier was captured while serving as a blockade runner. He served five months in federal prisons where he developed lung trouble, a handicap with which he struggled until his death at the age of 39.

After the war, Lanier married Mary Day in Macon in 1867, and they had four children. The city continued to serve as Lanier's home base. Many of the beautiful antebellum homes with which the poet was associated are still preserved here.

The Sidney Lanier Birthplace is a white wood-frame Victorian cottage with a gable roof. Built in 1840 as a simple four-room cottage with a small square stoop at the front entrance, the cottage has changed over the years. In 1879 a spacious porch with Victorian ornamentation was added. The roof was raised providing a second story with two large rooms. In the early 1900s a kitchen was added, as well as another downstairs room and an upstairs sleeping porch. In addition, exterior Victorian embellishments were replaced with a simple design more in keeping with the character of the original structure.

The interior decor is typical of the early 19th century. The original pine floors and four original fireplaces remain. Authentic period pieces and accessories are installed throughout the main floor, while historical reproductions are used for fab-

Lanier's birthplace, decked out for the Christmas season.

Poet and musician Sidney Lanier.

rics and carpets. The antique candlelight chandeliers, which have been wired for electricity, grace the main parlor and dining room. Lanier memorabilia, such as a portrait, silver flute, chair, and his wife's wedding dress, are displayed in the house.

The Sidney Lanier Birthplace also serves as headquarters for the Middle Georgia Historical Society. Hours are Monday to Friday, 9 a.m. to 1 p.m. and 2 to 4 p.m., and Saturday, 9:30 a.m. to 12:30 p.m.

ILLINOIS

—————————— Galesburg ——————————

■

CARL SANDBURG

Poet, biographer, historian, journalist, and minstrel—
Carl Sandburg was all of these. He was born in this cottage, which had been purchased by his father, August
Sandburg, for $365 in fall 1873—four years after arriving in Galesburg from Sweden and one year before
his marriage to Clara Mathilda Anderson. It was in this three-room cottage, located in the heart of an immigrant neighborhood, that the two eldest Sandburg children were born on cornhusk mattresses and diapered in flour sacks: Mary first in 1875 and then Carl in 1878.

Sandburg's birthplace was the second house east of the Chicago Burlington and Quincy railroad tracks. His father, who never learned to write, worked in the nearby railroad blacksmith shop for $1 a day, six days a week. His mother could read and write in both Swedish and English, but her life revolved around her husband and children. In 1879, one year after Carl was born, they sold the house and began a succession of moves to progressively larger homes. Between 1880 and 1893, five other children were born.

As the second of seven children, Carl was expected to supplement the family income, so he helped by delivering newspapers and working as an office boy. When he finished the eighth grade in 1891, he took on a full-time job as a milkman and later worked as a porter in the Union Hotel barbershop. In 1897 he spent five months as a hobo riding trains through-

Carl Sandburg.

out the West. In the process he learned many folk songs, the beginnings of his *American Songbag*. The following years he volunteered for the Spanish-American War and served briefly in Puerto Rico. Returning to Galesburg, he entered Lombard College, supporting himself by working as an on-call fireman. At Lombard he was greatly influenced by Philip Green Wright, a talented scholar and political liberal. Sandburg left Lombard

Carl Sandburg Birthplace, the first dwelling purchased by the poet's immigrant father.

before taking his degree, sold stereopticon viewers, and wrote for two years before his first book of verse, *In Reckless Ecstasy,* was published in 1904 through Wright's basement press.

Sandburg grew progressively more concerned with the plight of the American worker and became an organizer for the Wisconsin Social Democratic Party in 1907. At party headquarters in Milwaukee, he met Lilian Steichen, who became his wife a year later. He turned to journalism and worked on several Chicago newspapers. In 1914 his "Chicago" and other poems were published and won the prestigious Levinson Prize given by *Poetry Magazine.*

During the next five years, Sandburg wrote two more volumes of poetry, *Chicago Poems* and *Cornhuskers,* as well as a searching analysis of the 1919 Chicago race riots. More poetry followed along with *Rootabaga Stories,* a book of fanciful children's tales. The book prompted Sandburg's publisher, Alfred Harcourt, to suggest a child's life of Abraham Lincoln. Three years later Sandburg produced the two-volume *Abraham Lincoln: The Prairie Years,* by this time no longer a children's book. It was his first financial success and encouraged him to write a complete Lincoln biography. He moved to a new home on the Lake Michigan dunes and devoted the next few years to four additional volumes, *Abraham Lincoln: The War Years,* for which he won a Pulitzer Prize.

Sandburg continued his writing, publishing more poems, a second volume of folk songs, an autobiography, and a novel, *Remembrance Rock.* In 1945 the Sandburgs moved, with their herd of prize-winning goats and thousands of books, to Flat Rock, North Carolina (see Carl Sandburg Home National Historic Site, page 67). For *Collected Poems* he won a second Pulitzer Prize in 1951. Following his death in 1967, his ashes were returned to his native city.

The Carl Sandburg Birthplace reflects the typical living conditions of a working-class family over a century ago. Many of the furnishings belonged to the Sandburg family. A room was

Lindsay with his wife, Elizabeth Connor, whom he married in 1925, and their children outside the family home, c. 1930.

added to the rear of the cottage in 1949 to house exhibits and memorabilia.

Administered by the Illinois Preservation Agency and located in the southwest section of Galesburg, the site is open Tuesday to Saturday, 9 a.m. to noon and 1 to 5 p.m., and on Sundays, 1 to 5 p.m. It is closed on all state holidays.

────────── Springfield ──────────

■

VACHEL LINDSAY

Vachel Lindsay not only was born in this house in 1879, he grew up here and returned to it as his home base throughout his career. He brought his own family, including his wife, Elizabeth, and two small children, to live in the home in 1929, and he died here in 1931.

Lindsay, a major American poet, sought through his works to establish a new "localism" that was uniquely American, a voice that would express the folkways of the small towns and countryside. His poetry echoed the tastes and ideas representative of the agrarian frontier and the democratic, evangelical Midwest of the 1910s and 1920s.

During his lifetime he made long tours on foot, in the manner of the medieval troubadours, paying his way by reciting and trading his poems for food and shelter. In summer 1912 he walked from Illinois to New Mexico, distributing his poems and speaking on behalf of the "gospel of beauty." His poems, remarkable for their phonetic effects and rhythm, are more than drums and taps. He planned the architecture of each poem with definite effects and climaxes in mind.

The poem that first established his national and international reputation was published in 1913 and called "General William Booth Enters Into Heaven," following the death of the founder of the Salvation Army. He lectured at many universities, including Oxford and Cambridge in England. He was named resident poet at Gulf Park College in Gulfport, Mississippi, in 1923.

Sitting on a rise overlooking the governor's mansion and lawns, the Vachel Lindsay Home was built in 1846 by Henry

Vachel Lindsay, troubador and poet of the Midwest.

Dresser for Abraham Lincoln's sister-in-law, who often entertained the Lincolns here before the Civil War. Dresser had also designed and built the nearby home of Abraham Lincoln. Lindsay no doubt was much influenced by the proximity of so much history; he invoked the ghost of Lincoln in his famous poem, "Abraham Lincoln Walks at Midnight," which Carl Sandburg called "among the supremely great American poems."

After Lindsay's death by suicide, the home was retained in the family and eventually sold to the Vachel Lindsay House Fund by the heirs of his sister Olive.

The house, an Italianate structure, is filled with original fixtures and period furnishings. The walls are covered by a collection of artwork, writings, and dreams of the "Prairie Troubadour." Among the rooms are a main parlor with fireplace, grand piano, and combination bookcase and desk; northeast bedroom on the first floor where the poet was born; dining room with original dining table and chairs; and second-floor bedroom where the poet worked using a table and easel now on display.

The Vachel Lindsay Home, administered by the Illinois Historic Preservation Agency, is open Saturday only, 9 a.m. to 4 p.m., throughout the year.

—————————— Greenfield ——————————

■

JAMES WHITCOMB RILEY

James Whitcomb Riley, the Hoosier Poet, was born in a typical upper middle class house in 1849. This 10-room dwelling was an appropriate domicile for the family of a prominent attorney, Riley's father, who would be elected to the state legislature. Here, in this friendly house, "Bud," as Riley was called, learned to love the storytelling that was part of family life. All family members were great readers, and this instilled a love of reading that would last the rest of his life.

Riley's mother wrote poetry, some of which was published in the Greenfield paper, and no doubt she had an important influence on her son. When his mother died, Riley left the family home and traveled in Indiana and Ohio as part of a medicine show. Riley and his guitar entertained people throughout the two states with his own verses and songs.

Many of Riley's poems were written about his childhood memories, and his stories readily incorporate settings and descriptions of his birthplace. Here is the Riley family dining room "where they et on Sundays" and the rafter room, the horrible place where "the Gobble-uns 'll git you ef you don't watch out." Perhaps his best-known poem is "Little Orphant Annie," written about a real person named Mary Alice Smith. Visitors can see the side porch where Annie would "shoo the pigeons off the porch."

Riley's verse is marked by a rich native flavor, humor, and pathos. Always he wrote verses about what he saw and heard, even recording words exactly as they were spoken. This "di-

James Whitcomb Riley, famous for his use of dialect.

Birthplace of James Whitcomb Riley.

alect" writing was misunderstood, and it was some time before his work was accepted by the literary establishment, although it always attracted a popular following because of its
simple sentiments and sincerity. Eventually his poetry was
published in newspapers in Indianapolis and magazines
throughout the nation. Bobbs-Merrill, an Indianapolis publisher, published his books. For many years he traveled
throughout the United States reciting his poems to packed
houses.

The James Whitcomb Riley Birthplace was bought by the
city of Greenfield in 1935 and opened to the public as a historic home in 1937. It has been kept in good repair and was
restored in 1986. Administered by the Riley Old Home Society, the house is open May 1 to November 1, Monday to Saturday, 10 a.m. to 4 p.m., and on Sunday, 1 to 4 p.m.

■

JAMES WHITCOMB RILEY

Born in Greenfield in 1849 (see James Whitcomb Riley Birthplace, page 59), James Whitcomb Riley came to live in this house on Lockerbie Street in 1893. It was here with the Holstein family that the poet lived for 23 years until his death in 1916.

Riley had longed for a permanent home while traveling extensively on the lecture and entertainment circuit, and Indianapolis was a natural choice. One of his Indianapolis friends was Charles Holstein, an attorney and amateur poet. A warm friendship developed between the poet and the Holstein family, and the family invited the poet to live with them with the understanding that he would pay his share of the household

James Whitcomb Riley Home on Lockerbie Street, where Riley lived with the Holstein family

expenses. The living arrangement became permanent, and the next years were, perhaps, the happiest of Riley's adult life.

The Lockerbie Street house is an Italian Villa design built in 1872 — the exterior, plain and unpretentious, with a walk leading up a short grassy slope. A second walk curves to the side beneath the balustraded porch.

Inside the furnishings are sumptuous and suited to a well-

Entrance to Cabin in Wildflower Woods.

to-do Victorian family. Each room, including the room in which the poet died, has been maintained as it was when he lived there, displaying the comfort and elegance of the late 1800s. The house has been described as one of the finest Victorian restorations in the United States.

The wide hall includes half-paneled walls and a high ceiling with frescoes and a metal and etched-glass chandelier. Opening from the hall is a large, stately drawing room, its windows velvet-draped in gold and black with cornices of gold leaf. Chairs and sofas are ornate, overstuffed, and tasseled. The finest room in the house, the dining room, is spacious and hospitable, the furniture heavy and elaborately carved after 19th-century fashion. Walls are paneled and windows deeply set within glossy woodwork.

Riley's "nook" is an airy chamber on the second floor, carpeted, with a massive bed, Morris chairs, and a fireplace of mottled black marble. The poet installed a desk, shelves for his books, his pictures, a mask of Keats, the terra cotta of Dickens, and other prized belongings.

The James Whitcomb Riley Home, administered by the James Whitcomb Riley Memorial Association, is open Tuesday to Saturday, 10 a.m. to 4 p.m., and Sundays, noon to 4 p.m.

Rome City

■

GENE STRATTON-PORTER
Cabin in Wildflower Woods

Author and naturalist, Gene Stratton-Porter was born in 1863 at Hopewell Farm near Wabash, Indiana. Her father, Mark Stratton, an ordained minister, conducted services every Sunday at the little church at the corner of his farm. He inspired his daughter's love for and interest in wildlife, and the family farm became the classroom that fostered her lifetime avocation as an outstanding naturalist.

From her mother she learned the joys of a well-kept house, savory meals, gracious hospitality, and beautiful things to delight the eye. Like the rest of her 11 siblings, she was assigned household chores. The idyllic farm life ended when the family moved into the town of Wabash to be closer to a doctor because of her mother's poor health. School and city life were torture to the Stratton children after the freedom of the farm, where at-home tutoring had been the custom. An avid reader, Gene Stratton soon adjusted and became an able student. She was first encouraged to write when one of her book reviews received praise.

She met her husband, Charles Dorwin Porter, a druggist from Geneva, Indiana, at the resort of Sylvan Lake. An engrossing series of letters to each other led to marriage. The young couple's first home was in Decatur, where their only child, Jeannette, was born. Returning to Geneva, Porter's business affairs flourished, and the family soon was affluent enough to build a home — Limberlost Cabin in Geneva on the fringe of Limberlost Swamp. Here Stratton-Porter's early love of nature found a perfect laboratory for exploration and for writing.

In 1907, *At the Foot of the Rainbow* and *Wings* were published, followed two years later by *Birds of the Bible* and the book that was to make her a major American writer, *A Girl of the Limberlost*. It won such an immense world audience that it became the first American book to be translated into Arabic. Since then, her works have been translated into seven foreign languages.

Her beloved Limberlost Swamp was drained in 1913 by logging interests, and the destruction prompted the Porters to purchase 150 acres of land along Sylvan Lake. They built a new home, similar to Limberlost Cabin, and moved there in 1914. They turned the area, which they named Wildflower Woods, into a wildlife sanctuary.

Around this period, the popularity of Stratton-Porter's books led to a number of changes in her life. In 1919 she traveled to California to negotiate the rights to several of her books with film industry representatives. In order to be available for consultation, she purchased a small house there and began work on another book. In 1920 she decided to establish permanent

Gene Stratton-Porter with birthday bouquets, c. 1910.

residency in California, making regular visits to Wildflower Woods where her husband had remained. They maintained an amicable relationship until her death.

In the 21 years since her first book, she had completed 19 works, along with numerous articles and short stories. Hollywood had adapted three of her books for the screen. She continued to write, tend her Indiana garden, view the wild creatures on her visits to Wildflower Woods, and photograph. In November 1924 she was to spend the Thanksgiving holiday with her daughter in Los Angeles. Just a few blocks from her daughter's home, her car stalled and was struck by a streetcar. She never regained consciousness.

The Cabin in Wildflower Woods designed by Stratton-Porter lies nestled on the shores of Sylvan Lake, near Rome City. It is a two-story structure, with exterior walls of Wisconsin cedar logs. Local wild cherry was used to panel the entrance hall and dining room. Three fireplaces, one of polished English brick, one constructed of Indiana artifacts and stones from other states, and one of "pudding" stone, grace rooms in the cabin. Furnishings in the home are arranged and maintained to reflect as authentically as possible the Porters' lifestyle. Many original furnishings and memorabilia, including the author's library, are preserved.

Administered by the Indiana State Museum System, tours of the site, including the cabin, 20 acres of woods, trails, and the formal gardens, are conducted Wednesday through Saturday, from 9 to 11:30 a.m. and from 1 to 4:30 p.m., and Tuesday and Sunday, from 1 to 4:30 p.m. The site is closed on Monday.

————————— Gardiner —————————

■

EDWIN ARLINGTON ROBINSON

Born in 1869, Edwin Arlington Robinson moved to Gardiner when a young boy, living there until he attended Harvard University. He spent only two years at Harvard, returning to his hometown where he took on odd jobs but spent most of his time reading, writing, playing the

Edwin Arlington Robinson.

violin, and meeting friends as part of the Quadruped Club. These get-togethers centered around literary discussion and gave Robinson the opportunity to explore his own writings.

Many of Robinson's fictional characters were based on Gardiner personalities. His first collection of verse, *The Torrent and the Night Before,* was written and published while he lived here. His early poems attracted much critical attention for their originality and depth of exploration into the psychology and actions of his characters. With the publication of *The Man Against the Sky* in 1916, he received complete recognition as a major American poet. He won the Pulitzer Prize three times:

Robinson's boyhood home showing the large extension
off the house.

in 1921 for his *Collected Poems* and in 1925 and 1927 for his long narrative poems, *The Man Who Died Twice* and *Tristram*. He published several volumes of collected poems and two poetic plays. In 1929 he was awarded the Gold Medal of the American Academy of Arts and Letters. He also received honorary degrees from Yale University and Bowdoin College. He died in 1935.

The Robinson home, an example of a vernacular Italianate residence, was built before 1856 and remodeled in 1870. Double doors with lights of cranberry-colored glass open onto a narrow hall with double parlors to the side. Besides four bedrooms, the second floor boasts the first bathroom in town. A 1 ½-story ell extension contains the kitchen and woodshed as well as three bedrooms, the first of which belonged to Robinson. Two servants' rooms and a finished attic, which Robinson and his brothers used as a workshop, are included in the house.

The house is now owned by Barbara Robinson Holt, niece of the poet. Very few of the original furnishings survive, and the interior has been remodeled since the poet's time. The exterior, however, is largely unchanged. There are no specific visiting hours, but from time to time Elizabeth Calloway, daughter of the owner, conducts informal tours.

─────────── Portland ───────────

■

HENRY WADSWORTH LONGFELLOW

The Wadsworth-Longfellow House was the boyhood home of the poet, built between 1785 and 1786 by his maternal grandfather, General Peleg Wadsworth, as the first brick residence in this coastal city. Wadsworth settled in Portland after his service as an adjutant general of the Massachusetts militia during the Revolutionary War. He had been second in command of the disastrous expedition against the British at Castine, Maine, in 1779. The following year he was in command on the Maine coast with headquarters in Camden but was taken prisoner and carried to Fort George at Castine. From here he made an adventurous escape in 1781. In 1784 he determined to settle in Portland, buying this house from John Ingersoll for 100 pounds. He built a store and went into the general goods business.

Elizabeth Wadsworth, one of General Wadsworth's six children and mother of the poet, was married in 1804 to Stephen Longfellow in the parlor of this house, her home from early childhood. Ironically, while Henry Wadsworth Longfellow considered this his home until 1843, a period of 35 years, he was not born here. Rather, he was born in 1807 in a house owned by a paternal aunt who had asked the young Longfellow couple to move in with her during her husband's absence on a business trip to the West Indies. The poet was eight months old when his parents moved back to the Wadsworth house, where six of the poet's siblings subsequently were born.

Henry Wadsworth Longfellow lived here during his infancy, boyhood, and young manhood, and he often visited until the end of his life. His last visit, in June 1881, prompted him to write to a friend, "Portland has lost none of its charms. The weather is superb and the air equal to that of Newport or East Greenwich or any other Rhode Island seashore."

After graduation from Bowdoin College in 1825, where he was in the same class as Nathaniel Hawthorne and Franklin Pierce, he accepted a teaching position at Bowdoin, with the understanding that he spend some time in Europe studying modern languages. After three years he took up his teaching duties and two years later married Mary Storer Potter, also a native of Portland. The Wadsworth-Longfellow House continued to serve as his home base during this period. A good

Boyhood home of Henry Wadsworth Longfellow, built by his grandfather.

Henry Wadsworth Longfellow as a young man.

deal of his poetry was written in this house as well as a portion of the first of his two novels, *Hyperion*. (See Longfellow
Home National Historic Site, page 91.)

Today the house is administered by the Maine Historical Society, whose headquarters and library are adjacent to the residence. The 15-room Federal-style house contains furnishings
once belonging to and reflecting the lifestyle of the Wads-
worths and the Longfellows, including the four-poster bed of

the poet's great grandfather and the trunk the poet took on his first voyage to Europe.

A massive front door opens into a spacious hallway, which runs through the house to a rear door opening onto the garden. At the time the house was built, the parlor was the largest reception room in the city and contained the first spinet in town. The present piano was purchased by the poet for another house when he married and was used by the family for many years. It was sent here to replace the spinet, which had been disposed of. The parlor was the scene of many family festivities, including the marriages of the poet's own mother and two of his sisters. All but one piece of furniture here belonged to the Longfellows.

In the living, or sitting, room of the house is the table upon which the Longfellow children studied their lessons during winter evenings. Between the front windows stands the sewing table of the poet's mother. By another window is the poet's favorite chair and corner. The dining room was once General Wadsworth's "den," and it is here on the old schoolmaster's desk between two windows overlooking the garden that Longfellow wrote *The Rainy Day* in 1841.

The Wadsworth-Longfellow House is open June 1 to Columbus Day, Tuesday to Saturday, 10 a.m. to 4 p.m., and is closed July 4 and Labor Day.

South Berwick

■

SARAH ORNE JEWETT

arah Orne Jewett, who lived and wrote in this house for most of her life, brought the novel of local color to its highest degree of perfection in 19th-century American literature. She was born in South Berwick near the Piscataqua River in 1849 to a country doctor and grew up reveling in the New England countryside and the Piscataqua River. She took careful note of the landscape and its inhabitants as she accompanied her father on his rounds and incorporated her impressions in more than 40 novels and collections of short stories that capture the lives and landscapes of rural Maine in the late 19th century. Devoted to her father, she commemorates him in one of her early novels, *The Country Doctor.* She was educated locally and ended her formal schooling after graduating from the Berwick Academy.

Jewett's first published works were short stories under the pseudonyms Alice Eliot and Sarah O. Sweet. Shortly after, however, her works were readily accepted and she wrote under her own name. As she gained popularity, she also traveled more and gained exposure to life and society in Boston, New York, Philadelphia, and elsewhere. She developed friendships with editors and other authors, all of whom influenced and applauded her writing. Her best-known work, *The Country of the Pointed Firs,* was published in 1896.

Jewett's work attracted attention, not just for its subtle depiction of New England life, but also for its more universal themes concerning community life in the 19th century. While she is recognized as one of the 19th century's masters of the short-story form, her work is also valued for its historical perspectives. Toward the end of her life she wrote, "I have always meant to do what I could about keeping some of the old Berwick flowers in bloom, and some of the names and places alive in memory for with many changes in the old town they might soon be forgotten." She died in 1909.

The Sarah Orne Jewett House is considered an example of the exceptional craftsmanship and distinguished Georgian architecture of the colonial maritime community that settled along the Piscataqua River in southern Maine. Originally built for John Haggins in 1774, the modest exterior most likely was complete before the Revolutionary War, while the interior, with its ornately decorated woodwork, was paid for with the

Sarah Orne Jewett.

help of post-war profits. The house has a steep hipped roof
with flared eaves, a trademark of builders in the Portsmouth,
New Hampshire, area. A two-story ell, projecting from the
right rear of the house, contains the laundry and kitchen. The
entrance is a pedimented portico supported by two Doric
columns. Three dormer windows were added by Jewett and
her sister Mary in 1890.

A keystone arch with fluted pilasters supports the central

hallway leading to a carved staircase. Records indicate that two men worked for 100 days to complete the elaborate joinery in the front hall, including a distinctively carved newel post and a recessed window seat with paneling. Ornamental work in the house's four major rooms includes elegant wainscoting and cornices with a dentil pattern. Furnishings in these rooms include French flocked wallpaper, ornamental rugs, mahogany

House where Jewett spent most of her life. The dormers in the roof were added by the author and her sister.

tables and chairs, all representative of the Jewett sisters' decorative style of the late 19th century.

The author's own bedroom on the second floor remains as she knew it, with even the paint trim and wallpaper untouched since her death in 1909. Her desk stands in one corner with a portrait of her beloved father above it; her riding crops and skater's lantern hang above the fireplace; and her well-worn Bible sits on the nightstand.

The paint and wallpapers in several other rooms tell interesting stories. Family history indicates that the wallpaper in her sister's room was taken from a French ship brought into Salem, Massachusetts, by a privateer between 1750 and 1760. Intended for a French governor's house in the West Indies, it is an elaborate floral design of crimson velvet on a pink and white background speckled with mica. A hallway wallpaper is a recent reproduction of an English pattern documented in turn-of-the-century photographs of the house.

The Sarah Orne Jewett House, administered by the Society for the Preservation of New England Antiquities, is open June 1 to October 17, Tuesday, Thursday, Saturday, and Sunday, from noon to 5 p.m.

──────────────── Baltimore ────────────────

■

EDGAR ALLAN POE

Born to itinerant actors in Boston in 1809, Edgar Allan Poe lost both parents before the age of three. He was raised in Richmond, Virginia, by John Allan, a wealthy tobacco merchant, and his wife. He spent his youth with the Allans in England where he attended boarding school. Returning to Richmond, he enrolled in the University of Virginia, and, although he excelled in Latin and French, he was forced to withdraw when John Allan, angered by Poe's gambling debts, ended his support. At 18, Poe set off for Boston where he published his first volume of poems, *Tamerlane and Other Poems,* and enlisted in the army.

A brief reconciliation with his foster father led to an honorable discharge from the army and an appointment to West Point, but this, too, ended when John Allan remarried. Having no profession or financial support, Poe moved to Baltimore in 1829 hoping to earn a living as a writer. He lived with his aunt, Maria Poe Clemm, and her daughter, Virginia, in this house on Amity Street.

The little family scraped by in the cramped and inhospitable quarters. Entrance was by a steep staircase and Poe's garret space had a sharply pitched ceiling that rose only to about six feet near the center. The kitchen was six by ten feet, and at that time water had to be carried from Lexington Market, one-quarter mile away. During this period Poe felt particularly destitute, writing a last letter to his adoptive father beseeching him for

Amity Street house where Poe lived in cramped quarters with his aunt and cousin.

his assistance. But in the narrow third-floor garret that was his room for the next few years, Poe wrote some of his astute literary criticism and several short stories that formed the basis of his collection, *The Tales of the Folio Club*. One of these, "MS. Found in a Bottle," eventually brought him public attention in 1833 when it won a literary contest and a much-needed cash prize of $50, a generous amount for a contest then. Most important, it won the attention of one of the judges, who became Poe's benefactor. Through this connection, Poe was appointed to a post on a literary magazine in Richmond, Virginia, in 1835. He left Baltimore that year, marrying his cousin Virginia, then only 13, in 1836.

For the *Southern Literary Messenger*, he was responsible for a prodigious output of poems, stories, and critical reviews. But his bouts of drunkenness eventually cost him the position. The following year Poe, his wife, and Maria Clemm moved to New York City. (See Edgar Allan Poe Cottage, page 143, and Edgar Allan Poe National Historic Site, page 183.)

The Amity Street house once marked the western border of Baltimore but is now among a sea of houses. When a slum clearance project threatened to raze all structures on the street in 1938, the Poe Society protested and the street was saved. The house was leased to the Poe Society, then to the city's Commission for Historical and Architectural Preservation, which continues to manage the property.

Furnishing a house where Poe once lived always has been a challenge for house museums. Little remains of objects or furnishings that can be linked directly to Poe in any of his many residences, and Poe himself left scant evidence in his letters. He never kept a journal or diary. In restoring this house, duplicates of pieces that Poe might have used have been installed.

The Edgar Allan Poe Home is open April 1 to July 30, Wednesday to Saturday, noon to 3:45 p.m.; August and September, Saturday, noon to 3:45 p.m.; and October 1 to mid-December, Wednesday to Saturday, noon to 3:45 p.m. It is closed mid-December to March 30.

─────────────────── Amesbury ───────────────────

■

JOHN GREENLEAF WHITTIER

Whittier was born in 1807 near Haverhill, Massachusetts. His scanty education led him to read assiduously to educate himself; he was inspired particularly by the poetry of Robert Burns. His first poems were published in 1828 in the *Newburyport*

Home where Whittier lived with his mother, sister, and aunt.
Whittier's favorite spot for writing was called the Garden Room.

Free Press, edited by William Lloyd Garrison, the abolitionist, with whom he struck up a binding friendship. His first book, *Legends of New England,* appeared in 1831.

When a delegate to the National Anti-Slavery Convention in 1833, he began a lifelong commitment to the anti-slavery campaign to which he contributed personal aid as well as numerous essays and poems, culminating in 1835 with "Laus Deo," a poem acclaiming the final success of the anti-slavery program. He served in the state legislature in 1835 and held various editorial posts until his poor health compelled him to retire to his Amesbury cottage in 1840.

Although retired, he continued to write. An edition of his poems had appeared in 1837, to be followed by a full collection in 1849. He began contributing to the newly founded *Atlantic Monthly* in 1857, and volumes of poems appeared at two- and three-year intervals thereafter. His best-known book of poetry is *Snow-bound,* a charming picture of his boyhood home. The ballad form was Whittier's forte, and ballads such as "Barbara Fritchie," "The Barefoot Boy," and "Skipper Ireson's Ride" became popular favorites.

As a young man, several years after the death of his father, Whittier had been obliged to sell the old Whittier homestead in Haverhill. He moved to Amesbury with his mother, younger sister, and aunt, choosing a small house near the Friends Meeting House, which the family attended. Whittier wrote in the Garden Room of the Amesbury home for more than 40 years. At his death in 1892, after a funeral service in the house's garden, he was buried in the family lot in the Friends section of the Amesbury burial ground.

Although many additions have been made to the house since Whittier's death, the rooms and furnishings have been preserved much as they were during his residency.

The John Greenleaf Whittier Home, administered by the Whittier Home Association, is open May 1 to October 31, Tuesday to Saturday, 10 a.m. to 4 p.m.

John Greenleaf Whittier.

■

EMILY DICKINSON

The Dickinson Homestead played an especially crucial role in the experiences of Emily Dickinson and the formation of her poetry. The Mansion, as it was called, was her home for most of her life, and here she wrote most of her poetry and letters, tended her garden, baked bread, and generally helped to maintain the household.

Born in 1830, Dickinson led a quiet life. Her father, a lawyer, raised her following traditional Puritan New England values and sent her to two academies restricted to women. At 23 she accompanied her father, who had been elected to the U.S. Congress, to Washington, D.C., and while there she had a brief and mysterious affair that cast a tragic shadow over the remainder of her life. She returned to Amherst to live in seclusion the rest of her life.

Only seven of her poems were published in her lifetime, and her literary fame did not come until the appearance of a collection of her poems in 1890 and her letters in 1894. The poems, although uneven in quality, display a keen and original mind, questioning everything, tearing down traditional conceptions, and building anew. The best of her short lyrics rank with the best of modern poetry.

The Dickinson Homestead was built by the poet's grandfather, Samuel Fowler Dickinson, one of the founders of Amherst College, in 1813, and it passed into and out of the family's hands over the next few years. Edward Dickinson, the poet's father, added several rooms and constructed the cupola after repurchasing the house in 1855. At the poet's death in 1886, her younger sister, Lavinia, remained in the Mansion until her own death in 1899. After a series of owners, Amherst College bought the property in 1965.

The house now serves double functions as a college residence and as a historic landmark. For the most part, no attempt has been made to preserve the house as it was during the poet's life. One room, however,—Dickinson's bedroom on the second floor—has been re-created as her private sanctuary, emphasizing the scene of the poet's imaginative life and work. The poet's own writings and the memories of a niece provided the major sources of information about the room. A Franklin stove, cane chair, and sleigh bed, believed to have been the poet's, are displayed here, along with other family pieces. Most of the house's original furnishings have been dispersed; some are on display at the Houghton Library, Harvard

Homestead of the Dickinson family. One room has been dedicated as a memorial to the poet.

University, including the poet's writing table and the bureau in which she stored much of her poetry, written on scraps of paper and discovered only after her death.

The Dickinson Homestead is open by appointment May through October, Wednesday to Saturday, 1:30 to 3:45 p.m., and in early spring and late fall on Wednesday and Saturday only. It is closed December 1 to March 1.

Emily Dickinson, most of whose works were discovered after her death.

■

WILLIAM HICKLING PRESCOTT

lthough outdated by current research, the works of William H. Prescott, one of the greatest of American historians, are still valued for their style and narrative quality. Born in Salem, Massachusetts, in 1790, Prescott graduated from Harvard University and entered his father's law office but was compelled to abandon law because of a serious eye injury. After receiving medical attention in Europe, he resolved to devote himself to historical writing and began work on *The History of the Reign of Ferdinand and Isabella,* published after 10 years' work and to much acclaim.

Next followed his most popular work, *History of the Conquest of Mexico,* published simultaneously in Boston and London in 1843. Because of his eye injury, Prescott could not travel, making the accuracy and descriptions of his foreign scenes just that much more remarkable. He relied on reference material purchased both here and abroad, scholars whom he hired to do research in foreign collections, and American diplomatic and consular officials and traveling friends to provide the necessary background and insight.

In 1844 Prescott purchased this house on Beacon Hill where he would write *The Conquest of Peru* and live during the remaining 15 winters of his life. The house and the twin structure next door, built in 1808 on land once owned by the painter John Singleton Copley, are the only surviving structures from the early 1800s that overlook Boston Common. The Georgian exterior is much the same as it was in Prescott's day.

The present dining room was Prescott's library, with walls once covered with embossed polychrome leather and dark oak bookcases. Here had hung the crossed swords of Prescott's and his wife Susan's grandfathers, both of whom had fought in the Revolutionary War but on opposite sides. Colonel William

Engraving of William Hickling Prescott by D. J. Pound showing the nearly blind historian using his famous octograph.

Prescott had cautioned his men at Bunker Hill, "Don't shoot until you see the whites of their eyes," while Captain John Linzee commanded the British warship that shelled Bunker Hill. While on a visit with the Prescotts, William Makepeace Thackeray was inspired by the story to write *The Virginians*. The swords are now at the Massachusetts Historical Society.

Prescott's home, now a house museum as well as headquarters for the National Society of the Colonial Dames of America in Massachusetts.

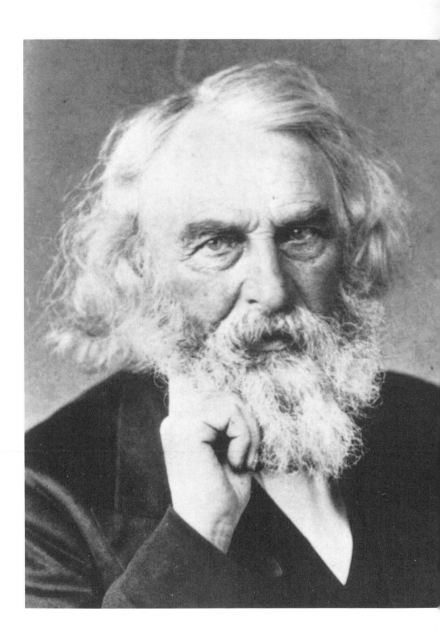

Henry Wadsworth Longfellow, American poet and literary scholar, in his later years.

Prescott's study on the top floor has been faithfully restored by the National Society of Colonial Dames of America in Massachusetts, which uses part of the house as its headquarters. The restoration was documented using an original woodcut illustration in George Ticknor's *The Life of Prescott*. Contained in the room, among other objects, are wood panels over each of six windows to control the light that bothered Prescott's sensitive eye, a small English desk with its sloping lid, and an octograph, an instrument invented by a member of the Wedgewood family in England to enable a writer with little or no sight to write legibly in a straight line.

The house includes fine collections of export trade porcelain and English ceramics and costumes from the 18th century to the present. It is open every Wednesday throughout the year, 10 a.m. to 4 p.m., except on holidays.

──────────────── Cambridge ────────────────

■

HENRY WADSWORTH LONGFELLOW

The rich history behind the Longfellow Home National Historic Site involves two important personalities — the legendary poet, after whom the house is named, and George Washington, who used this residence as his headquarters during the siege of Boston in the Revolutionary War. Here, also, George and Martha Washington celebrated their 17th wedding anniversary in January 1776. Longfellow, who had installed a bust of Washington in the house, once wrote, "When you come to Cambridge, you will find George Washington brought down from his station on the stairs, and standing in the hall below, where he can be better seen. In his place you will see an Old Dutch clock, whose silver chimes will lull you to sleep at night. At the half-hours, it strikes the coming hour to give timely warning. The hours are struck on a larger bell and the chimes 'shiver the air into a mist of sound.'"

The poet first lived here as a boarder in 1837 after accepting a post at Harvard University. But before taking up his full-time duties, he traveled again to Europe to study German (see Wadsworth-Longfellow House, page 70). In Rotterdam, his wife of seven years died after a miscarriage. The bereaved poet returned to Cambridge to teach and take up permanent residence. He married Frances (Fanny) Elizabeth Appleton in 1843, and his new father-in-law purchased the house for the couple, who had six children here. Resigning his professorship in 1854, he devoted the rest of his life to writing and enjoying the fame that increasingly came his way. He received honorary degrees from Cambridge and Oxford universities; his bust is in Westminster Abbey's Poet's Corner, the only American poet so honored.

The second half of the 19th century marked the blossoming of literature in all its forms in New England. The Brahmins in Cambridge and Boston, the transcendentalists in Concord, and the abolitionist writers throughout New England were the people with whom Longfellow conversed and corresponded. These were the men and women who fostered an American literary tradition. They wrote from experiences uniquely shaped by life in the United States, a young nation that was manifestly proud of its accomplishments yet too weak to correct the flaws in its social fabric and that would soon be entrenched in a long and painful civil war.

Longfellow's friendship with Charles Sumner, a United States senator from Massachusetts and an ardent opponent of slavery, most likely prompted his own *Poems on Slavery* in 1842, one of Longfellow's infrequent forays into contemporary politics. Generally, however, the poet stayed away from political issues and remained a part of the world of letters. Aside from receiving scathing criticism from Edgar Allan Poe, Longfellow's work was admired and respected throughout North America and Europe. His poetry struck a responsive

Longfellow Home National Historic Site, witness to events surrounding George Washington as well as the beloved poet.

chord in people's hearts and minds, and his readers genuinely loved him.

For 45 years, until his death in 1882, Longfellow lived in this Greek Revival house on Brattle Street. Here he wrote his most famous poetry, such as "The Children's Hour," "The Ride of Paul Revere," and "The Village Blacksmith," and received visitors from around the world. Originally built in 1759 for Major John Vassall, a wealthy Tory who fled Cambridge on the eve of the Revolution, the house was purchased in 1791 by Andrew Craigie who added the piazzas and a rear ell. To pay his debts, Craigie's widow was forced to take in lodgers, one of whom had been Longfellow.

The house was occupied by Longfellow descendants until 1913 when the Longfellow House Trust was formed in order to preserve the residence "as a specimen of the best colonial architecture of the middle of the 18th century, as a historical monument of the occupation of the house by General Washington and as a memorial to Henry Wadsworth Longfellow."

A massive front door with a large brass knocker greets visitors to the house. On the landing in the hallway is the ornate 17th-century Dutch clock alluded to by Longfellow above. Numerous portraits hang throughout the house. The study, to the right of the hallway, is the room used by Washington as his office and later by Longfellow as his study. From July 1775 to April 1776 Washington held conferences in this room with his generals and once received a committee headed by Benjamin Franklin. Three months after his departure the Declaration of Independence was signed. The room is preserved, however, as Longfellow's study, and everything has been left as it was at the time of the poet's death: his Hepplewhite armchair, the folding desk opened as if about to be used, his quill pen, the green china inkwell, the inkstand bearing the inscription *Saml Taylor Coleridge:his inkstand,* from which Coleridge had written the "Rime of the Ancient Mariner." To the right of the fireplace stands the armchair made of wood of the "spreading chestnut tree," presented to Longfellow by the children of Cambridge on his 72nd birthday in 1879. It has been painted black and carved with the forms of horse chestnut leaves; lines from "The Village Blacksmith" are inscribed around the base. The library, changed somewhat after Longfellow's death, contains the poet's extensive collection of works by Greek poets and dramatists and 19th-century French and Italian poets. The library probably had originally served as a dining room and was used as a ward room and officer's mess by Washington's staff. Finally, the garden, described by Longfellow as "a small garden in the form of a lyre," is behind the house and was enlarged later following a design he had seen on a visit to Italy.

The Longfellow Home National Historic Site, including the house, is administered by the National Park Service of the U.S. Department of the Interior. It is open daily except Thanksgiving, Christmas, and New Year's Day from 10 a.m. to 4:30 p.m.

■

LOUISA MAY ALCOTT
Orchard House

The daughter of Amos Bronson Alcott, an advocate of educational and social reform, Louisa May Alcott was born in Germantown, Pennsylvania, in 1832. Soon after, her father established his Temple School in Boston, and the family moved with him to Massachusetts. Early in life, Alcott found it necessary to help support her family and tried domestic service, sewing, teaching, and, at 17, the stage. She wrote several melodramatic plays. Her first book, *Flower Fables*, published in 1854, was a collection of tales written for Ralph Waldo Emerson's young daughter. By 1860 her poems and short stories began to be published in the *Atlantic Monthly*, and her writing proved to be a major source

Orchard House, the setting for Alcott's well-known *Little Women*.

Louisa May Alcott, whose love of writing was demonstrated early in life.

of income for her progressive but struggling family.

During the Civil War she was a nurse in the Union Hospital in Georgetown, now part of Washington, D.C. Her letters written to her family during that period were published as *Hospital Sketches*. Her first novel followed in 1864.

Her father's idealism and that of her early teachers, Henry Thoreau and Emerson, combined with her own energy and delight in life in her books. She sought material and characters among her own family and friends, capturing a sense of spontaneity and freshness especially evident in her most famous work, *Little Women*, published in 1868 as her second novel.

Orchard House is the setting of this well-loved book. The house is really two dwellings, both built around 1700, combined by Alcott's father after purchasing the 12 acres on which they stood in 1857. Bronson Alcott added gables and porches to the houses and rustic garden structures to the property, setting the stage for the lives of a unique 19th-century family with special gifts in the fields of literature, the arts, and philosophy: Abigail May, his wife, active in prominent social issues of the day, including women's rights, abolition, and welfare of the underprivileged; Anna, the eldest daughter, an accomplished amateur actress; Louisa, the most widely known of the Alcotts; May, a talented artist and early teacher of sculptor Daniel Chester French; and, last, himself, founder of the Concord School of Philosophy situated on the hillside behind the house. The Concord School flourished as a summer school for adults until his death in 1888 and, today, continues to be the site of educational programs. Louisa May Alcott also died in 1888, the same year as her father.

Administered by Friends of the Alcotts, Orchard House contains many of the furnishings original to the family, and work continues to restore many rooms in the house, including reproducing original wallpapers and paints. The house is open from early April to mid-September, Monday to Saturday, 10 a.m. to 4:30 p.m. On Sundays, holidays, and from mid-September through late October, it is open from 1 to 4:30 p.m.

■

RALPH WALDO EMERSON

Poet, essayist, and philosopher, Ralph Waldo Emerson was born in Boston in 1803 to William Emerson, a descendant from generations of New England clergymen. The younger Emerson's early years were taken up with books and a daily routine of home life that included morning prayers, spelling lessons before breakfast, Latin and writing instruction, chores, and evening devotions. His aunt, Mary Moody Emerson, assumed responsibility for his training in the Emerson family tradition. In 1817 he entered Harvard University, and in 1825 he began divinity school also at Harvard.

Although he took up a position as minister of Old North Church in Boston in 1829, the same year he married Ellen Tucker, he felt uncomfortable with the conformity expected under traditional religious practices and beliefs and resigned as pastor in 1832. By this time his wife had died of tuberculosis. Seeking better health himself, he went abroad in 1833, traveling throughout the Mediterranean, England, and France. While on this voyage he met some of England's great writers

Ralph Waldo Emerson, from an 1854 daguerreotype.

whose beliefs had a strong effect on Emerson's own tendency to transcendentalism. He did not enjoy life as a tourist and returned home to begin his work as a lecturer. In 1835 he bought his Concord home and moved into it with his second wife, Lydia Jackson of Plymouth, and his mother.

Emerson achieved fame for his writings based on his transcendental philosophy, which espoused the importance of individual intuitive belief and harmony with nature. He lectured widely and edited *The Dial*, a magazine that provided a forum for transcendental ideas. His first collection of poems appeared in 1847, and several collections of his lectures followed. In the 1850s he became absorbed in anti-slavery issues,

Emerson's home, which set the stage for many gatherings of the transcendental writers and thinkers of New England.

and at the outbreak of the Civil War rejoiced to see a national spirit called forth to combat slavery. Although his mental capacity declined during his last decade, these years were brightened by expressions of affection and respect shown by his friends and townspeople. He died in 1882.

When Emerson first moved here in 1835, he was not a newcomer to Concord, having lived at the Old Manse on Monument Street, built by his grandfather in the mid-18th century. Soon after moving into the house, Emerson added a parlor and bedroom, the "Straw Carpet Chamber," to the house giving the house its distinctive squarish shape, and in 1857 he made further alterations. Four children were born to Emerson and his wife here, one of whom died at the age of eight. The three remaining children, Ellen, Edith, and Edward, grew up here. The guest chamber on the ground floor, called by Emerson the "Pilgrim's Chamber," was the room where the children were born so that the convalescing mother would not need to climb stairs.

Many famous men and women of the day visited Emerson

Henry David Thoreau in a photograph taken well after his Walden Pond retreat.

in this house. Henry Thoreau stayed here during two winters when Emerson was away. Nathaniel Hawthorne, William Ellery Channing, Amos Bronson Alcott and his daughter Louisa May Alcott, all were familiar faces. In the evenings, a group of these thinkers and writers occasionally gathered in the parlor. Emerson himself was apt to go for long walks in the woods near Walden Pond, returning to write the results of his meditations and observations in his study.

One night in 1872, a servant upset a lamp, setting the house on fire. None of the children was at home, and neighbors helped to save most of the house's contents. While the attic was destroyed, the main structure was not badly damaged. The Emersons moved to the Old Manse until the house could be repaired. A few days later, a group of friends presented the family with several thousand dollars toward repairing the damaged house. While this work was going on, Emerson and his wife went abroad and returned in summer 1873 to find the house made over and much improved. Here they lived until Emerson's death in 1882 and his wife's in 1892, when Ellen Emerson took charge of the house until her own death in 1909.

The Ralph Waldo Emerson House, administered by the Ralph Waldo Emerson Memorial Association, is open April 16 to mid-October, Thursday to Saturday, from 10 a.m. to 4:30 p.m., Sunday, from 2 to 4:30 p.m., and holidays 1 to 4:30 p.m.

■

HENRY DAVID THOREAU
Cabin at Walden Pond

Henry David Thoreau was born in 1817. He was one of the most original geniuses in the group of New England transcendentalists, which included Ralph Waldo Emerson, Margaret Fuller, and Nathaniel Hawthorne. His own extreme individualism led him to oppose the philosophy of the group.

Replicas of Thoreau's cabin on the grounds of the Thoreau Lyceum and installed at Walden Pond.

Absorbed from childhood in the study of nature, he made collections at the age of 12 for the noted Swiss naturalist Jean Agassiz. His unique and impetuous temperament made it impossible for him to pursue a scientific career, and throughout his life he worked only when in need of money.

In 1845 he retired to a cabin he had built on the shores of Walden Pond in Concord, living there in solitude for two years and two months so that he could study nature and write. His journal from this experience was published in 1854 as *Walden, or Life in the Woods,* one of the classics in American literature.

In this volume, as in subsequent writings, he expressed his philosophy of individualism and extolled the right of man to withdraw from civilization and the conventions of society. He wrote, "I went to the woods because I wished to live deliberately, to front only the essential facts of life, and see if I could not learn what it had to teach, when I came to die, discover that I had not lived."

After Thoreau's retreat ended in July 1847, ownership of the cabin reverted to Ralph Waldo Emerson, who owned land on which the cabin stood. The cabin subsequently was sold and relocated several times before it was dismantled as building material to repair other structures. Two replicas of the cabin exist: one built by the Thoreau Society and erected at the Thoreau Lyceum in Concord and another by the Massachusetts Department of Environmental Management at the entrance to Walden Pond State Reservation, about one-half mile from the original site. Both replicas include reproductions of Thoreau's bed, his desk, and one of his chairs.

The Thoreau Lyceum, which includes a research library and a permanent collection of memorabilia as well as changing exhibitions, is open daily from April 1 to December 31; Thursday to Sunday from January 1 to February 15; and Tuesday to Sunday from February 16 to March 31. Hours are weekdays and Saturday, 10 a.m. to 5 p.m., and Sunday, 2 to 5 p.m.

The Walden Pond State Reservation is open daily throughout the year from 5 a.m. to dusk.

■

WILLIAM CULLEN BRYANT

William Cullen Bryant was born in 1794, not in this house, but in a gambrel-roofed cabin of rough-hewn lumber two miles from the then-frontier village of Cummington. The second of seven children of Peter and Sarah Snell Bryant, he was five years old when his family came to live here, the home of his maternal grandfather.

Under the guidance and criticism of his father, Bryant began to write verse as early as his fifth year. To prepare him for entrance in Williams College, he received further schooling from the Reverend Moses Hallock as well as his father. After

William Cullen Bryant.

a year at Williams, he left to study law and was admitted to the bar in 1815.

His most famous poem also firmly established his reputation as a poet. "Thanatopsis" was published in the *North American Review* in 1817, before Bryant turned 23. In 1829 he became editor-in-chief of the *New York Evening Post* and in 1849 joint owner with John Bigelow. Under Bryant's control, the newspaper became an advocate for the Union and supported anti-slavery issues. As the editor of the leading journal of opinion, he introduced Abraham Lincoln to an influential audience at Cooper Union in New York City. The impression Lincoln made there helped propel him into office on the eve of the Civil War.

Bryant was a tireless campaigner. In New York he campaigned for a paid fire department, a uniformed police force, and paved sidewalks. He championed the establishment of Central Park. He knew virtually everybody of importance in America and met most of Europe's famous personages as well. He became wealthy, owning a town house in New York City and a country estate in Roslyn on the north shore of Long Island. A rousing orator always in demand throughout his life, his death occurred as a result of a public appearance in 1878: During a lengthy speech in Central Park on a hot day, he fainted, striking his head on a stone. He lingered for some days. (See William Cullen Bryant's Cedarmere, page 157.)

The William Cullen Bryant Homestead, built in 1785 by his grandfather, passed through several owners before Bryant purchased his boyhood home in 1865. He rebuilt the wing that had served as his father's medical office, using this as his study, and raised a section of the south end of the house to provide room for a first-floor parlor and dining room. What is now a Palladian window on the second floor of the south wall had been a front door. The house now is a Dutch Colonial style with Italianate ornamentation.

Much of the furniture and many of the decorative objects in the house are believed to have been there when Bryant lived in the house as a boy and in his later years. According to tra-

William Cullen Bryant Homestead, substantially altered by the author after he purchased it in 1865. The house originally had been built by Bryant's grandfather in 1785.

dition, the dining room chairs and table probably were part of the house's furnishings when Bryant was growing up. The tall-case clock in the parlor is a wedding present to Frances Fairchild on her marriage to Bryant in 1821. On the stairway to the second floor, the cast-iron bracket lamp and its ornate globe are original to the house. A large Second Empire maple tall-post bed dominates Bryant's bedroom, across the hall from that of his wife. At the foot of the bed is a leather-bound trunk, which Bryant took on his travels, and on this is a basket containing two wooden dumbbells, used by the editor and writer every morning as part of his vigorous physical fitness regimen.

The William Cullen Bryant Homestead, administered by the Massachusetts Trustees of Public Reservations, is open from the last weekend in June through Labor Day, Friday to Sunday, 1 to 5 p.m., and from Labor Day to Columbus Day, Saturday and Sunday, 1 to 5 p.m.

■

EDITH WHARTON
The Mount

Edith Wharton was born in 1862 to a socially elite family in New York City. Typical of the Victorian era, she received a private education. She was an omnivorous reader, and by age 11 she was attempting to write her own novels, but her parents regarded such an occupation with suspicion. At a suitable marriageable age, she wed Edward R. Wharton, a Boston socialite, in 1885. Only a few years as a society matron convinced Wharton to turn to other occupations. She began to travel widely, to exercise a talent for decorating, and, ultimately, to write.

During long stays in Europe she developed a keen appreciation for classical architecture, leading to her *The Decoration of Houses* in 1897, written with Ogden Codman, Jr., the architect, and *Italian Villas and Their Gardens* in 1904, books that became touchstones of taste in their day and continue to influence architects, designers, and gardeners.

Her novels chronicle turn-of-the-century society and won the admiration of her peers such as Henry James, with whom she was good friends, as well as William Dean Howells, André Gide, Sinclair Lewis, and Aldous Huxley. During her lifetime she wrote 21 novels and novellas, 11 collections of short stories, nine books of nonfiction, and numerous articles and reviews. In 1920 she became the first woman to win the Pulitzer Prize, awarded for her novel *The Age of Innocence*. Two of her most popular novels, *Ethan Frome* in 1911 and *Summer* in 1917, document the landscape around her home, The Mount. Wharton died in France in 1937.

The Mount was built in 1901 and designed by Wharton following her own advice in her book on decorating. She had the assistance of Ogden Codman and architect Frances L. V. Hop-

The Mount, Wharton's unique creation in the Berkshires of western Massachusetts.

pin, as well as her niece, the landscape architect Beatrix Farrand, who helped her lay out the terraced gardens and vistas. This three-story Georgian structure was modeled after a 17th-century English country house and is unusually sited against and over an outcropping of rock, giving the effect of bringing the landscape up to the house. The site is a balanced composition consisting of the house, the Red Garden, named for its blossoms in deep red and maroon colors, and the Italian Walled Garden.

To Wharton, the gardens were the most important feature of the site. In July 1911 she wrote, "Decidedly, I am a better landscape gardener than novelist, and this place, every line of

Edith Wharton at her writing desk.

which is my own work, far surpasses *The House of Mirth,"* her novel set in the landscape of The Mount. The gardens were a source of inspiration for a number of her novels. From her bedroom window she could look down on this green land-scaped world and people it with her fictional characters.

In 1971 the estate, administered by the Edith Wharton Restoration, was made a National Historic Landmark, and ex-tensive restoration was begun. Fortunately, both the house and grounds have survived with no significant alterations to the original 1902 design. The house and its 50-acre setting retain their original beauty and architectural interest. Henry James, a frequent guest, noted "the charm of this admirable house" and described it as "a delicate French chateau mirrored in a Massachusetts pond."

The Mount is on Plunkett Street and is open Memorial Day weekend to Labor Day, Tuesday to Sunday, 10 a.m. to 5 p.m.; after Labor Day to October 31, Thursday to Sunday, 10 a.m. to 5 p.m. It is closed November until Memorial Day weekend.

—————————————— Pittsfield ——————————————

■

HERMAN MELVILLE
Arrowhead

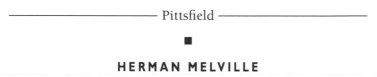

Born in 1819 in New York City, Herman Melville signed on the whaler *Acushnet* when he was 22 and sailed out of New Bedford, Massachusetts, for a three-year voy-age to the South Seas. His adventures in the Marque-sas, Tahiti, and other Pacific islands provided much material for his early popular romances, such as *Typee: A Peep at Polynesian Life* in 1846 and *Redburn* in 1849. By 1850 he was a promising young writer of 31 and ready to move his young family from New York City to a quiet location in which to con-centrate on his writing.

Arrowhead, so named by the author because of the number of arrowheads he unearthed as he plowed the soil.

He chose Pittsfield, Massachusetts. Here he acquired 150 acres and a fine 18th-century farmhouse in the Berkshire hills of western Massachusetts. In 1850, with a loan from his father-in-law, chief justice of the Massachusetts Supreme Court, Melville, his wife, Elizabeth, and their infant son moved into the house along with the author's widowed mother and his four unmarried sisters.

He bought the home for two reasons: to finish his novel *Moby Dick* and to be near a new and important friend, Nathaniel Hawthorne. The two men had been introduced at a picnic; Melville had just read a collection of Hawthorne's stories, *Mosses from an Old Manse*, and had written rhapsodically about them, comparing the author to William Shakespeare. Hawthorne, in turn, was captivated by Melville and invited him to his cottage near Lenox.

Melville named his property Arrowhead after the Indian artifacts he plowed up in the fields in his attempt to farm the land. The house had been built in 1780 on land that once belonged to the Mohicans. Because it was sited on the post road between Hartford, Connecticut, and Bennington, Vermont, for many years it had been run as an inn.

He wrote *Moby Dick* all that winter in 1850 and much of the next year. It finally was published in 1851 but was not well received by the public, who failed to grasp the author's symbolism and the book's deep philosophical underpinnings. Ironically, the work is now considered one of literature's masterpieces.

Melville farmed the land but plowed only enough to raise crops for a horse and cow and to plant a garden. For the most part he was preoccupied with writing. He wrote every day from about 9 a.m. to 2:30 p.m. in a large second-story bedroom he had made into his study. His writing table faced a north window with a view of Mount Greylock. A bookcase full of the classics stood to one side. A harpoon served as a poker. To a friend in New York City he wrote, "I have a sort of sea-feeling here in the country, now that the ground is all covered with snow. I look out of my window in the morning as I would out of the port-hole of a ship in the Atlantic. My room seems a ship's cabin and at nights when I wake up and hear the wind shrieking, I almost fancy there is too much sail on the house and I had better go on the roof and rig in the chimney."

Melville lived at Arrowhead for 13 years, completing *The Confidence Man, Pierre,* and *The Piazza Tales* here. He developed other close literary friendships with Berkshire residents including Oliver Wendell Holmes, David Dudley Field, and the Sedgewick family.

Failing to attract a large number of readers, Melville's books provided insufficient income to support his family, so he turned to writing shorter pieces for magazines. Money trou-

Herman Melville, as photographed by Rodney Dewey in 1861.

bles intensified when, in 1853, a warehouse fire destroyed all unsold copies of his books, and income from them ceased. His declining health led to a trip to Europe and the Holy Land in 1856 with the support again of his father-in-law. Arrowhead was closed, and the family dispersed for the winter.

On his return, Melville tried to make a living as a traveling lecturer, but his subjects were too serious to be popular. He looked for, but could not find, a buyer for Arrowhead and a steady job. Finally, in 1863, his brother Allan took over the property, giving Melville a small house on East 26th Street in Manhattan. Three years later, at the age of 47, Melville began work as a customs inspector in New York City, a post he kept for 19 years. He died six years after retiring in 1891, a few months after finishing one last great work, *Billy Budd*. Few newspapers carried his obituary.

Arrowhead's Chimney Room, which inspired one of the author's short stories.

Arrowhead stayed in his brother's family until 1927. After a series of owners and many changes, the property was acquired in 1975 by the Berkshire County Historical Society. Despite the many renovations the building has undergone in the last 200 years, the early colonial floor plan remains. Its stout chimney, 12 feet square at the base, rises through the center of the house radiating heat from its fireplaces to the rooms surrounding it. The author's study, the piazza, the "chimney room" fireplace he featured in his short story "I and My Chimney," and the barn in which Melville and Hawthorne spent many hours discussing their work are all open to the public.

Arrowhead, a National Historic Landmark, is open Memorial Day to October 31, Monday to Saturday, from 10 a.m. to 4:30 p.m., and on Sunday, from 11 a.m. to 3:30 p.m. After Labor Day it is closed on Tuesday and Wednesday.

──────────────── Salem ────────────────

■

NATHANIEL HAWTHORNE

This novelist and short-story writer was born in Salem in 1804 in a simple two-story structure typical of New England houses of the period. Originally sited at 27 Union Street, the house was moved in 1958 to a historic site, joining the House of Seven Gables, built in 1640 and the only remaining 17th-century mansion in New England, Hooper-Hathaway House, built in 1682, and Retire Becket House, built in 1655, all administered by the House of Seven Gables Settlement Association.

Hawthorne, the son of a ship captain, lived here only 10 years, when his mother, widowed when the author was four, moved to Raymond, Maine. He remained in Maine for a number of years, going to Bowdoin College and spending 12 years in solitude developing his writing. In 1828 his first book, *Fan-*

Nathaniel Hawthorne.

shawe, a college romance, was published but to little acclaim. He won an audience through his short stories, however, and in 1837 these were collected in *Twice-told Tales*. Not long afterward, *The Tales of a Grandfather's Chair* appeared. During 1839 and 1840 he worked as a measurer in the Boston customhouse at an annual salary of $1,500. When his job was ter-

Hawthorne's birthplace on the site of the House of Seven Gables.

minated, he invested $1,000 in an experiment in communal living in Roxbury, Massachusetts, called Brook Farm. Here he lived doing chores as a plowman and "barnyard-dressing spreader." The experiment, which had attracted other New England writers interested in transcendentalism, was not suited to Hawthorne, although it is through this experience that he met his wife, Sophia Peabody. They married in 1842.

Needing better income to support his wife and daughter Una, Hawthorne took another customhouse position in 1845, this time in his native city, where he remained for some time writing his greatest work, *The Scarlet Letter*, published in 1850. During a temporary sojourn in 1851 in Lenox, Massachusetts, he wrote *The House of Seven Gables*, the setting of which was his cousin's house in Salem where he was a frequent visitor. Both stories capture the brooding, dark New England environment for which Hawthorne is famous.

His association with Franklin Pierce, whom he had known at college, led in 1853 to a position as consul in Liverpool, England, for four years. He then traveled throughout the continent, concentrating on Italy, and in Florence he wrote *The Marble Faun*. After seven years in Europe he returned to a wartorn United States. He died in 1864 on a trip to the White Mountains in New Hampshire with Pierce.

The Nathaniel Hawthorne Birthplace was built by Benjamin Pickman before 1685, although some historians date it no earlier than 1740. It is furnished as it would have been when Hawthorne was born. The site is open daily, 9 a.m. to 5 p.m., except Thanksgiving, Christmas, and New Year's Day.

—————————————————— Niles ——————————————————

■

RING LARDNER

Midwestern humorist Ringgold Lardner was born in 1885 and raised in this Gothic Revival house at 519 Bond Street. Private tutors provided his early education, but he graduated from Niles High School in 1901. Four years later he became a newspaper re-

Lardner's boyhood home, now a multi-family dwelling.
An expansive Victorian porch was removed some time ago.

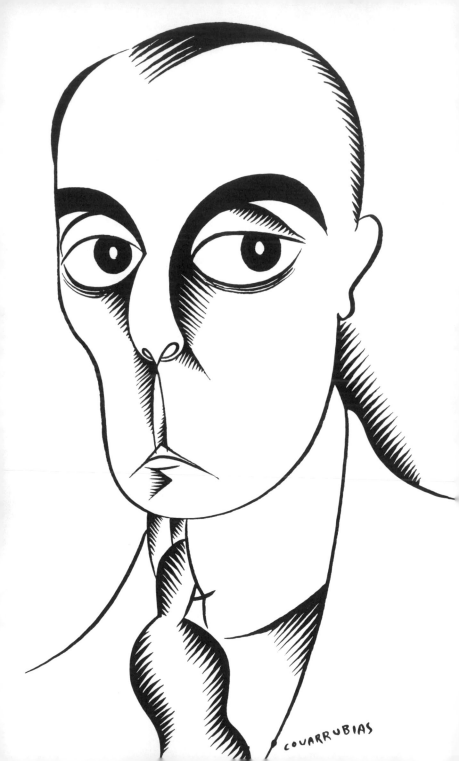

porter for the *South Bend Times,* later becoming its sports reporter. In 1907 he moved to Chicago to continue his sports writing for newspapers there. With the publication of his first book, *You Know Me, Al,* in 1916, he became a popular and recognized short-story writer. His play *Elmer the Great* had a long stage run and was produced as a movie.

Lardner's sports experiences served as the background for most of his writings, especially a popular series of stories called *The Busher's Letters,* published originally in the *Saturday Evening Post* and later collected in a book. He joined other Midwestern humorists as a caustic but sympathetic portrayer of naive American character, and his sarcastic bent is evident in most of his writing. He died in Long Island, New York, in 1933, after a long bout with tuberculosis.

The Ring Lardner Home was built in the late 1860s by R. C. Payne, the town banker and later its mayor. The two-story stucco dwelling has a gable roof and ornamental scrollwork. Around 1940 the house was converted to a multi-family dwelling with 17 rooms and three fireplaces. While much of the interior has changed, the ornamental woodwork remains very much as it was when the author lived here. Once graced by a generous Victorian porch, the house now has no porch and includes a small blocklike addition.

Privately owned, the home is not ordinarily open to the public, although the exterior can be viewed easily.

Humorist Ring Lardner, a caricature by Miguel Covarrubias published in *Vanity Fair* in 1925.

─────────── Sauk Centre ───────────

■

SINCLAIR LEWIS

Sinclair Lewis was born in 1885 in Sauk Centre, the youngest of three sons. His father, Edwin J. Lewis, a physician, was a stern and dictatorial man of Welsh ancestry, while his mother, Emma Kermott Lewis, was the daughter of a Canadian physician. Lewis was six years old when his mother died of tuberculosis. One year later his father married Isabel Warner, who encouraged his interest in literature.

At Yale University, Lewis began to write and contributed stories, poems, and articles to the *Yale Literary Magazine,* of which he became editor. His first fiction was published nationally in *Pacific Monthly.* For two summers he worked his way to England on cattle boats. He interrupted his college career to become a janitor at Upton Sinclair's experimental socialist community in New Jersey, Helicon Home Colony. Drifting to New York City, he tried his hand at freelance writing but returned to Yale and graduated in 1908.

Following graduation he crisscrossed the United States drifting in and out of various jobs with magazines and newspapers. A story in *Redbook* enabled him to go to California, where he worked as a secretary to two novelists in Carmel. There he lived with his old Yale classmate, William Ross Benet, and met many of the West Coast literati, including Jack London to whom he sold several story plots and for whom he was a ghostwriter.

After a stint in Washington, D.C., with various magazines, he found his place in the working world of New York City. He

Sinclair Lewis on Main Street in 1947.

Lewis's boyhood home, now part of a larger site that includes
a schoolhouse.

was a manuscript reader for two years and later editorial assistant and advertising manager for the George C. Doran Company. Under the pseudonym Tom Graham, he wrote his first
book *Hike and the Airplane,* an adventure story for boys published in 1912. Other novels followed, but until 1920, Lewis
was an undistinguished storyteller. It was in 1920 that Lewis
published the novel he had been thinking about for 15
years — *Main Street.* This satire of small-town life in the Midwest brought the author instant success. It sold nearly one
million copies, was translated into many foreign languages,
and made Lewis an international figure. Other equally suc-

cessful works followed in this decade: *Babbitt, Arrowsmith, Elmer Gantry,* and *Dodsworth.*

In 1930, the same year his son Michael was born, he received the Nobel Prize for Literature, the first American to receive this honor. After this period, his work seemed to decline. He could not recapture the quality of the novels of the 1920s. All in all, Lewis wrote 23 novels and many short stories and plays, several of which he himself acted in. Fourteen movies were based on his writings. He married twice, but both marriages ended in divorce. He died alone in Rome, Italy, of pneumonia, after having suffered several heart attacks during the months before his death. His ashes were brought home to Sauk Centre and buried in the family plot at Greenwood Cemetery in January 1951.

Lewis was born in the small white house directly across the street from his boyhood home, into which he moved when he was four years old. The nine rooms of the boyhood home, including his father's medical office, have been carefully restored to the period when Lewis and his parents lived here. Wherever possible the original furnishings are used in conjunction with donated period pieces.

The Sinclair Lewis Boyhood Home, part of the Sinclair Lewis Interpretive Center, includes a visitor center, a schoolhouse, and the Lewis grave site. The house is on Sinclair Lewis Avenue and is open Monday to Friday, Memorial Day to Labor Day, 8:30 a.m. to 5 p.m., and the rest of the year, Monday to Friday, 8:30 a.m. to 2 p.m.

─────────────── Oxford ───────────────

■

WILLIAM FAULKNER
Rowan Oak

Generally regarded as one of America's most distinguished 20th-century novelists, William Faulkner was born in New Albany, Mississippi, in 1897 and spent most of his life in nearby Oxford. His parents were from old and respected southern families, and his schooling was informal. He read extensively, however, and undertook a regimen of self-study. He attended a public high school and the University of Mississippi but graduated from neither.

During World War I he served in the British Royal Air Force, then worked at odd jobs back in the United States, and drifted to New Orleans where he began to write for a magazine. An early novel published in 1929, *The Sound and the Fury,* attracted favorable attention, and, encouraged by its modest success, Faulkner bought a decaying house in Mississippi he called Rowan Oak. The name for the house was inspired by the legend of the Rowan tree, recorded in Sir James Frazier's *The Golden Bough.* The secluded two-story antebellum mansion was built in 1844 by Robert Sheegog, a planter and merchant in Oxford. Twenty years later, the house survived the Union raiders who put a torch to the city.

From 1930 through 1951, Faulkner produced almost a book a year while living here. And for 32 years, from the day he acquired it until his death in 1962, he gradually restored the house to its former beauty. He worked on the house as profits

Rowan Oak as seen down the cedar-lined path.

Faulkner's work area, added to the house between 1950 and 1952.

from his writings came in and as time permitted. With a local carpenter, Faulkner handled much of the renovation himself.

In 1950 Faulkner was awarded the Nobel Prize for Literature, and in 1955 he was awarded his own country's highest literary honor, the Pulitzer Prize, for his novel *A Fable*. Another Pulitzer was awarded posthumously in 1963 for his last novel, *The Reivers*.

Typical of the homes in the area, Rowan Oak stands at the end of a walk lined with ancient cedars. Outbuildings include a barn, kitchen house, and tenant house. Faulkner enlarged the original house, adding several rooms, and landscaped the grounds.

As you enter the house, Faulkner's work area, the library, is to the left. It contains personal artifacts and painted portraits of his family. To the right is the parlor with the Chickering piano that belonged to Estelle Faulkner, the author's wife. Faulkner's funeral was held here.

Photographs and portraits of special interest are on display in the back hall, which served as the Faulkners' sitting room.

The author's principal work area, a room added between 1950 and 1952 off the back hall, has been left as it was at the time of his death. His Underwood portable typewriter rests on a table near the window, and in the corner stands a small fold-top desk he made. Upstairs are the four family bedrooms.

Rowan Oak, now administered by the University of Mississippi, is open Tuesday through Saturday, 10 a.m. to noon and 2 to 4 p.m., and Sunday, 2 to 4 p.m.

Portrait bust of William Faulkner by Leon Koury.

————————— Red Cloud —————————

■

WILLA CATHER

Born in Winchester, Virginia, in 1873, Cather was almost 10 years old when her family moved to Nebraska in 1883, moving in with Cather's grandparents on their farm northwest of Red Cloud. A year later, the family moved into this house, which they rented for 20 years in town in order to take advantage of better schools, to be close to doctors for Cather's mother, who was ill, and to facilitate her father's farm loan business.

Cather lived here for six years until her graduation from high school when she attended the University of Nebraska in Lincoln. While in Lincoln she launched her writing career with reviews for the *Lincoln Journal,* although she had spent her youth expecting to be a doctor. She returned to Red Cloud after college graduation for only one year, before moving to Pittsburgh to teach and edit a magazine. From Pittsburgh she went to New York in 1906 for a position with *McClure's Magazine,* and it was in this city that she fully realized her potential as a novelist. She first won wide attention with her novel *O Pioneers!* in 1913, followed by others: *Song of the Lark* in 1915, *My Antonia* in 1918, and *Death Comes to the Archbishop* in 1927. *One of Ours,* a war novel published in 1922, won the Pulitzer Prize. She died in 1947.

In a 1921 interview, Cather noted that between the ages of eight and 15, a writer "unconsciously gathers basic material" for later work. That is especially true of this author and her novels, many of which deal with the western experience and

Historic view of the Cather home in Red Cloud.

at least six of which are set in the Red Cloud of her remembered youth with three of these giving detailed descriptions of parts of this modest house.

The Willa Cather Historical Center, part of the Nebraska State Historical Society, comprises six restored buildings that interpret the life and works of the author. The Willa Cather Childhood Home has been restored to the period of the author's occupancy and to the description of the house in her writings. A vernacular Greek Revival dwelling with a gable roof, it was built c. 1879 and has been repainted in its original light brown color. The Victorian front porch probably dates from the 1880s.

Other buildings at the site include St. Juliana Falconieri Catholic Church and Grace Episcopal Church, both of which figured in *My Antonia*. An interpretive center houses artifacts and archival collections about the author. The site enables visitors to see the places that made an indelible impression on the young writer; one can walk the streets and prairies that Cather knew and captured forever in her work.

The site is open May to September, Monday to Friday, 8 a.m. to noon and 1 to 5 p.m., and Saturday and Sunday, 1 to 5 p.m. From October to April, hours are the same, but the site is closed on Monday only.

---------- Derry ----------

■

ROBERT FROST

enowned poet Robert Frost was born in San Francisco in 1874, but his family's roots were in New England. Frost's mother, Isabell Moodie Frost, moved with her two children, Robert and Jeanie, to Lawrence, Massachusetts, in 1884 after her husband's death in order to operate a private school. It was from his father, however, that Frost inherited a love for distant lands and outlying farms. He wrote later, "My father could hardly pass an abandoned farm without wanting to own it."

Frost came to Derry in 1900 with his wife and former child-

Robert Frost Farm, site of the poet's early attempts to farm and write for a living.

Poet Robert Frost.

hood sweetheart, Elinor, and their baby daughter, Leslie. He was 25 years old and the period was a difficult one for him. His four-year-old son had just died of cholera, and his mother was terminally ill with cancer. In addition, he had just dropped out of Harvard University after only two years—a second and final attempt at a college education. His disappointed grandfather could not understand his unambitious grandson but, nevertheless, gave him the Derry farm, hoping he could manage as a farmer.

Frost did farm the land. For 10 years he made a living of sorts, raising poultry and teaching part time at Pinkerton Academy in Derry Village. As time went on he became more occupied with poetry and less with farming. Three more children were born here as well.

In 1911 Frost sold the farm and with the proceeds sailed for England with his family. He was unknown and virtually unpublished. A London publisher became enthralled with his work and published his first two volumes of poetry, *A Boy's Will* and *North to Boston*, in 1913 and 1914. They were quickly acclaimed on both sides of the Atlantic, and Frost was hailed as the leader of a new era in American poetry. When Frost returned to the United States in 1915, his reputation had been established.

From 1915 until his death in 1963, Frost wrote and read his poetry to many audiences, stimulated generations of students, and received honors throughout the world. He was awarded four Pulitzer Prizes for his poetry and received more than 50 honorary degrees, including degrees from the two institutions from which he had failed to graduate, Harvard and Dartmouth College.

The years he spent at the farm in Derry influenced all of his poetry. He wrote, "You might be interested to know that during my 10 years in Derry, the first five of them farming altogether and the last five teaching, but still farming a little, I wrote more than half my first book, much more than half of my second and even quite a little of my third though they were not published till later."

Although Frost later bought other farms (he once owned five at one time), the Derry farm held a special place. He was appalled to find the farmhouse being used as a garage with an automobile junkyard spreading into the fields in later years. He was, however, unable to reclaim the property.

The state of New Hampshire acquired the farm in 1965 and has since restored it to its turn-of-the-century condition. The poet's daughter, Leslie Frost, guided the restoration of the two-story white clapboard farmhouse, selecting furnishings representative of the few things the family owned. Original family paintings and photographs adorn the walls, and the dishes in

the dining room are authentic. On the grounds, the orchard, barn, and brook with its wildflowers — all reflected in Frost's poetry — have been restored. A short nature trail leads through the woods. At the south end of the property is the famous Mending Wall, inspiration for one of Frost's most-quoted lines.

Administered by the New Hampshire Division of Parks and Recreation, the Robert Frost Farm is open in the summer, Wednesday to Sunday, 10 a.m. to 6 p.m., and on spring and fall weekends, 10 a.m. to 6 p.m.

Portsmouth

■

THOMAS BAILEY ALDRICH

Thomas Bailey Aldrich was born in this house, the home of his grandfather, on Court Street in 1836, and he lived here until he was two years old when he and his family moved to New Orleans. He returned to Portsmouth in 1849 to live again with his grandfather and attend Portsmouth Academy until 1852. This period is best remembered in his most popular work, *The Story of a Bad Boy,* published in 1870 and the first realistic depiction of a boy in American literature.

His first literary success came at age 19 with the publication in 1855 of a sentimental poem, "The Ballad of Babie Bell." He was thereafter active in New York City's literary and artistic circles, making friends with leading cultural figures. He was a lifetime friend of Edwin Booth, brother of Abraham Lincoln's assassin.

He moved to Boston in 1865 where he succeeded William Dean Howells as editor of the *Atlantic Monthly.* His circle of

Thomas Bailey Aldrich, whose *The Story of a Bad Boy* captured the spirit of American boyhood.

friends in that city included Henry Wadsworth Longfellow, James Russell Lowell, and Mark Twain. It was here that he wrote his famous novel, the realism of which had a profound influence on Twain and his portrayal of Tom Sawyer.

Aldrich died in 1907 at the age of 70, by which time the house of his birth had passed out of the family. In the 1880s it had served as Portsmouth's first hospital. Repurchased by the Aldrich family, it was the first house in Portsmouth and one of the first in the United States to be restored to a specific period of its past. Mark Twain was among those who journeyed

Aldrich's home, now part of Strawbery Banke.

to Portsmouth for its dedication as the Thomas Bailey Aldrich Memorial.

In his lifetime Aldrich had nicknamed his grandfather's house the "Nutter House." It was built in 1797 by William Stavers, son of John Stavers, who operated the famous Pitt Tavern next door. Thomas D. Bailey, Aldrich's grandfather and a Portsmouth merchant, purchased the house in 1830. The house today reflects the author's boyhood of the mid-1800s and is almost exactly as Aldrich depicted it in *The Story of a Bad Boy:*

"Imagine a low-studded structure, with a wide hall running through the middle. At your right hand, as you enter, stands a tall black mahogany clock, looking like an Egyptian mummy set up on end."

That is how Aldrich began his description of the house. He continues, taking his readers on a tour of "large rooms wainscotted and rich in wood carvings about the mantelpiece. . . . walls covered with pictured paper representing landscapes and seascapes." Artifacts of those who lived here are still present, including the Bible in the parlor, where his grandfather would sit on Sunday reading aloud, and a shotgun and coat in the author's own bedroom.

The Thomas Bailey Aldrich Memorial Association kept the house open to the public for 71 years until 1979 when it became part of Strawbery Banke, a 10-acre outdoor history museum that has restored some 20 buildings dating from 1695 to 1945, most on their original sites. Strawbery Banke is one of America's oldest continuously occupied neighborhoods.

The Aldrich house is open as part of Strawbery Banke, May 1 to October 31, 10 a.m. to 5 p.m.

——————————— Camden ———————————

■

WALT WHITMAN

Walt Whitman was the poet of democracy. He wrote of working people, of the steam and sweat of the city, and of the rich loamy smells of the hills and the salty air along the shores of Long Island. His long tours on foot of the West and into Canada as a youth instilled in him a vision of the immensity of America and the dignity of the individual man within a democracy. In his poetry he sought to express a truly American experience, one that reflected the values and virtues, wishes and fears of the young American nation.

The "Good Grey Poet," born in 1819, happened to come to Camden near the end of his life. Around 1873, Whitman's mother became ill while visiting her son, Colonel George Whitman, the poet's brother, at his home on Stevens Street in Camden. Hearing that she was ill, Whitman, despite his own infirmities, traveled to Camden from Washington, D.C., where he had worked at the Department of the Interior, which had dismissed him because of his work in *Leaves of Grass,* and at the Department of the Treasury, where he had remained until a paralytic stroke left him partially disabled. Whitman stayed with his mother until her death. He continued to live with his brother, paying room and board, until 1884 when he purchased the house on Mickle Street, where he was to stay until his death in 1892.

The gradual success of *Leaves of Grass* enabled Whitman to purchase this house on Mickle Street, and the Lay family, then

Walt Whitman, as photographed by George C. Cox in 1887.

boarders, continued their residency at the house providing the poet with his meals. After the family's departure in 1885, an acquaintance, a sea captain's widow named Mary O. Davis, became his housekeeper and remained until his death. Whitman was buried in Harleigh Cemetery in Camden, in a secluded wooded section not far from the main gate. Most of the members of his family are also buried here. (See Walt Whitman's birthplace, page 145.)

Administered by the New Jersey State Park Service, the Walt Whitman House, a small two-story rowhouse, includes historic exhibits relating to Whitman's life and work and is open Wednesday to Friday, 10 a.m. to 6 p.m.; Saturday, 10 a.m. to 5 p.m.; and Sunday, 1 to 6 p.m.

Town house purchased by Whitman as his last residence.

——————————— Bronx ———————————

■

EDGAR ALLAN POE

In 1840, Edgar Allan Poe, then a noted but struggling poet and writer, moved from the crowded New York City environs he disliked to the more healthful and purer air of the village of Fordham, a section of the Bronx. He paid John Valentine a yearly rent of $100 for a wooden cottage built around 1812. The move, however, failed to save his young wife, Virginia, from the ravages of tuberculosis. She died in a small bedroom of this cottage in early 1847. Her death drove the poet into a fit of melancholy. His mother-in-law and a friend nursed him back to health.

Poe continued to live at the cottage for another two years, writing less frequently but still producing such works as "Ulalume," "Annabel Lee," and "The Bells," and endeavoring to establish a literary magazine over which he would have complete editorial control. Writing to a potential financial backer in Illinois, he gave an outline of his plans indicating the cost of the journal would be five dollars apiece with a circulation of 20,000.

During this period he continued to find intellectual stimulation from students and teachers at nearby St. John's College, today, Fordham University. Stimulation of another sort was found in the village taverns nearby, which he visited often.

Leaving the cottage in 1849 to begin a lecture tour on behalf of the magazine project, Poe traveled to Philadelphia and then to Richmond, the city of his childhood. While there he renewed his acquaintance with a boyhood sweetheart, Sarah Elmira Royster, whom he planned to marry. He left Richmond at the end of September intending to return to the Fordham cottage to collect his belongings and return south.

He never reached New York. A few days later he was found, semiconscious, lying outside a polling area in Baltimore, dressed in clothes that were not his. Because of the condition in which he was found, some believe he was plied with liquor and used as a repeating voter, a common practice in the notoriously corrupt political environment of that city during this era. The true circumstances of Poe's death remain a mystery. Friends brought him to Washington College Hospital where he lay in a delirium until his death four days later.

After Poe's residence at the cottage, several other tenants followed. By 1895 the tiny village of Fordham was already part of New York City. New houses were built, the population

Poe's cottage in the Bronx, where he sought to escape the close environs of Manhattan.

soared, and the cottage was threatened with demolition. The New York Shakespeare Society led efforts to save the cottage, and, in 1902, the city created Poe Park across the street and, in 1913, saved the cottage itself. The cottage was restored and refurbished to resemble its appearance when Poe lived there. (See Edgar Allan Poe Home, page 78, and Edgar Allen Poe National Historic Site, page 183.)

Administered by the Bronx County Historical Society, the Edgar Allan Poe Cottage is open Wednesday to Friday, 9 a.m. to 5 p.m., Saturday, 10 a.m. to 4 p.m., and Sunday, 1 to 5 p.m. It is closed in January.

Huntington

■

WALT WHITMAN

The Whitman family first settled in the Huntington area of Long Island in the mid-17th century. The poet was born in 1819 in this simple shingle-sided house, built by his father, Walter Whitman, Sr., sometime during the second decade of the 19th century. The year of the poet's birth, the senior Whitman moved his family to Brooklyn, New York, so he could find better work as a house builder to support his growing entourage.

Whitman attended grammar school in Brooklyn and took his first job as a printer's devil, or apprentice, for the *Long Island Patriot*. By 1835 he was employed as a printer in New York City. An economic depression forced him to return with his mother, father, his brother George, and sister Hannah to Long Island where he commenced a series of teaching positions and took up farming. In addition, he pursued his interest in newspapers. In 1838 he founded a weekly newspaper, *The Long Islander*. A year later he sold the paper and returned to New York City, only to return in 1840 to teach school and work for the *Long Island Democrat*. For the next 18 years he held positions on seven different newspapers, and it was during this period that he published the first edition of *Leaves of Grass*, 12 poems written in free verse praising the concept of universal love. Unable to find a publisher, Whitman himself hired a Brooklyn printer to print the verses in 1855. This first edition met with little critical approval, although Ralph Waldo Emerson recognized its worth and wrote a congratulatory letter to Whitman. Several editions followed, enlarged and revised, until Whitman's death in 1892.

In 1862 Whitman left Brooklyn to search for his brother George, listed as missing after the Civil War's Battle of Fredericksburg but who had been taken prisoner by the Confederates. During his search, Whitman was shocked by the plight of the wounded in military hospitals. He secured a civil service post in Washington, D.C., and, in his spare time, made nearly 600 hospital visits to tend to the wounded. He also continued to write, producing another volume of poetry related to his war experiences, *Drum Taps*, published in 1865. Eventually he lost his civil service position because of the controversy surrounding *Leaves of Grass*.

After the Civil War, Whitman remained in Washington with the Department of the Treasury until he suffered a paralytic stroke that partially disabled him. He eventually moved to Camden, New Jersey (see Walt Whitman House, page 141), where he remained until the end of his life.

Whitman's birthplace is an excellent example of native Long Island craftsmanship, simple in line and pleasing in proportion. Constructed of hand-hewn logs held together by wooden pegs, it is set on a base of roughly hewn whole tree trunks tied together by wooden pegs and supported on a foundation of small boulders. The structure is covered with cedar shingles. Notable architectural features include the corbeled chimney, storage closets in the fireplace walls, slanted wainscoting on the staircase, and large windows that provide light, air, and a rare note of elegance for a country farmhouse.

Walt Whitman's birthplace, a vernacular residence that represents the skills of local house builders.

The kitchen wing appears to be older than the main part of the house and may have been the original house to which the larger main section was added. Whitman's mother was of Dutch descent, and the graceful mantels in the parlor and another room have a convex curved shelf, a common treatment at the time among Dutch houses near New York City. The grounds around the house have undergone enormous change. A single acre remains from the sprawling fields and orchards once worked by Whitman's forebears. A single barn stands as a reminder of the corn cribs, hog pens, hay ricks, and other outbuildings long since replaced by wide lawns and huge shade trees.

The Walt Whitman House is administered by the Walt Whitman Birthplace Association. The site is open year round, Wednesday to Friday, 1 to 4 p.m., and Saturday and Sunday, 10 a.m. to 4 p.m.

■

THEODORE ROOSEVELT

This four-story reconstructed brownstone stands in what is now a business district—a far cry from the trim and respectable residential neighborhood that saw the birth of the 26th president of the United States, Theodore Roosevelt, in 1858. Roosevelt's grandfather built this and an adjoining house for his two sons in 1854, the same year that Roosevelt's father, Theodore, Sr., brought his southern bride, Martha Bulloch Roosevelt, to live here at 28 East 20th Street. Although the town house was neither large nor lavish by the day's standards, it was adequate for a young couple of moderate means. For the next 14 years it was the family home and the place where Roosevelt's sisters and brother were born.

Roosevelt passed his early formative years in the house. When he was 10, the family went off for their first grand tour of Europe. When Mrs. Roosevelt and the children returned to New York in late 1873, they moved into a new home on 57th Street. Roosevelt's birthplace remained in the family until 1896. As the neighborhood became more commercial, the house underwent a series of alterations until finally it was demolished. In 1919, the year of Roosevelt's death, a memorial association, encouraged by Roosevelt's two sisters, raised funds to buy the land and reconstruct the house, buying as well the adjoining property that had once belonged to Roosevelt's uncle. In 1923 the reconstruction was complete, including compatible office space built in place of the adjoining house.

The front entrance to the brownstone is reached by climbing a flight of stairs over the English basement. The first floor includes a parlor and library off a side hall, with a dining room running the full width of the house at the rear. Three bedrooms are on each of the next two floors with servants' quar-

Roosevelt's reconstructed birthplace. He lived at this address until he was 10 years old.

ters on the fourth floor. A special feature of both Roosevelt homes was the wide porch in the back overlooking the rear gardens. A door on these second-floor porches connected the two houses.

Theodore Roosevelt once wrote of his birthplace, "It was furnished in the canonical taste of New York, a period in which men of substance liked to have their homes reflect the dignity and solidarity of their traditions and their lives. The black hair-cloth furniture in the dining room scratched the bare legs of the children as they sat on it. The middle room was a library, with tables, chairs, and bookcases of gloomy respectability." (See Sagamore Hill, page 153.)

Administered by the National Park Service, U.S. Department of the Interior, the Theodore Roosevelt Birthplace National Historic Site is open Monday to Friday, 9 a.m. to 5 p.m.

---------------------------------- North Hills ----------------------------------

■

CHRISTOPHER MORLEY
Knothole

Essayist and novelist Christopher Morley was born in Haverford, Pennsylvania, in 1890. He published his first book while still a Rhodes scholar at New College, Oxford University in England. On returning to this country, he settled in Roslyn, New York, and was soon a familiar figure throughout the literary world. While he thought of himself as a poet, he was a columnist, dramatist, actor, journalist, critic, and author. His column was "The Bowling Green," for the *Saturday Review of Literature,* where he also worked as an editor. He served for nearly 30 years as a judge for the Book-of-the-Month Club. He was involved in two theatrical ventures: one in Hoboken, New Jersey, where old-fashioned melodrama was revived, and the other in Roslyn, New York, at the Mill-

Living room of the Knothole, Christopher Morley's retreat in the woods. Morley's portrait is above the fireplace.

pound Playhouse. He delighted in gathering kindred spirits and formed them into durable clubs such as the Baker Street Irregulars and the Three-Hours-for-Lunch Club.

He built the Knothole as a work area and retreat in 1934. "I built it myself as a pine-wood cabin," he wrote, "as aloofly jungled as a Long Island suburb would permit, to consort with the shade of John Bartlett." It soon became the site for meetings with friends and a prodigious amount of work. Besides revising and enlarging Bartlett's *Familiar Quotations* here, he wrote more than 50 books, including *Parnassus on Wheels, The Haunted Bookshop, Where the Blue Begins, Thunder on the Left,* and the best-selling *Kitty Foyle.*

Shortly after Morley's death in 1957, a group of neighbors formed the Christopher Morley Knothole Association for the purpose of preserving his studio, which was presented to

Nassau County in 1966 as the focal point of Christopher Morley Park.

The interior of the Knothole remains as it was, with built-in bunks still available for quiet reading, its friendly fireplace with a tea kettle on the hob, and, nearby, the huge writing table complete with papers, pipe, and an inkwell. The building also has a unique architectural feature—a "dymaxion" bathroom, a one-piece, pre-assembled unit designed by physicist and inventor Buckminster Fuller in the late 1930s. The browsing area features copies of Morley's books. Other books, letters, documents, and memorabilia are on display.

Located in the northeastern corner of Christopher Morley Park, which is administered by the Nassau County Department of Parks and Recreation, the Knothole is open weekends May to August, noon to 4 p.m., as well as extra days in July and August, Wednesday to Friday, 10 a.m. to 2 p.m.

—————————— Oyster Bay ——————————

■

THEODORE ROOSEVELT
Sagamore Hill

Our 26th president was a prolific writer of an astonishing number of very readable books. From 1877 until his death in 1919, Theodore Roosevelt is credited with writing more than 2,000 works covering American history, hunting, wildlife, and politics. His best-known writings are *The Naval War of 1812*, published in 1882, the biographies of Thomas H. Benton and Gouverneur Morris, *African Game Trails* in 1910, a result of a long trip in the Congo, *Winning of the West*, four volumes published between

Theodore Roosevelt, writer, rancher, conservationist, horseman, hunter, historian, and U. S. president.

1889 and 1896, *Through the Brazilian Wilderness* in 1914, another adventurous account of a trek through Brazil, and his own *Autobiography,* published in 1916.

As a young man Roosevelt determined that a public career was an attractive course for a bright and civic-minded person such as himself. Politics was the logical means to such a career. He joined the Republican Party in his district and with its help was elected to the New York State Assembly. While there he gained a reputation as a reformer, fighting against the social and economic injustices of the New York City slums. When, in 1884, both his wife and mother died, he left politics and went west to the Little Missouri River in Dakota country to become a rancher. After two years he returned to New York

Sagamore Hill, Theodore Roosevelt's estate on Long Island.

and accepted an appointment to the Civil Service Commission offered him by President Benjamin Harrison. In 1895 he became the New York police commissioner and left that post to become assistant secretary of the navy with the McKinley administration.

Roosevelt is fondly remembered especially for his role with the Rough Riders, who fought in Cuba during the Spanish-American War in 1898. He helped raise funds for this group of volunteers and fought with them at the famous Battle of San Juan Hill. Upon his return to New York, he was elected governor, promptly making himself unpopular with party regulars by attacking and taxing big business. Republican political figures were glad to push him as the country's vice president in 1900 and thus escape the wrath of influential New York City business interests. Only a few months into the vice presidency, Roosevelt assumed the presidency upon the assassination of William McKinley. His leadership of the country between 1901 and 1909 was bold and beneficial. He passed a food and drug act; established a department of commerce and labor to fight the trusts; helped fix railroad rates; and made possible the building of the Roosevelt, Hoover, and Grand Coulee dams in the West. He established a forest service dedicated to conservation and facilitated the construction of the Panama Canal. And the public liked him for his humor, his vitality, and his enthusiasm.

Seeking a third term as president in 1910, the Republican party ticket was split between Roosevelt and William Howard Taft. The three-way race left Woodrow Wilson as president. Forced to retire, Roosevelt continued to speak out on political issues and continued an active life at Sagamore Hill.

The Roosevelt home, Sagamore Hill, was built by Roosevelt between 1884 and 1885 and was his permanent home for the rest of his life. Five of his children were born here. As the "Summer White House," it served as host to numerous national and international figures from every walk of life. Theodore Roosevelt died here peacefully in 1919 from a heart embolism.

Engraving of William Cullen Bryant writing in his library
at Cedarmere. The Delft tiles around the fireplace survived
a devastating fire in 1903.

His wife, Edith, remained until her death in 1948. (See Theodore Roosevelt Birthplace, page 148.)

The name of the estate came from the Sagamores, a Native American tribe of the region. It is a rambling, solidly built 22-room Victorian structure of frame and brick, even now little changed since the Theodore Roosevelt era. On the first floor are a large center hall, a library that served as Roosevelt's private office, a kitchen, and a spacious north room added in 1905 according to a design by Roosevelt's friend, C. Grant La Farge, son of artist John La Farge. This 30-by-40-foot room is built of Philippine and American woods: mahogany, black walnut, swamp cypress, and hazel. It is crammed with hunting trophies, flags, and furniture, all reflecting the interests and spirit of its occupant.

The second floor includes the family bedrooms, a nursery, a guest room, and a bathroom with a great porcelain bathtub. Numerous other rooms in the house include servants' quarters, classrooms for the children, and the bedroom of Theodore Roosevelt, Jr., as it was in his pre-college days. Furnishings throughout the house are original pieces.

On the south and west sides of the house is the spacious piazza from which Roosevelt looked out over Oyster Bay Harbor and Long Island Sound. It was on this piazza that Roosevelt was formally notified of his nominations as governor of New York in 1898, as vice president in 1900, and as president in 1904 after winning his first full term.

The Sagamore Hill National Historic Site is administered by the National Park Service of the U.S. Department of the Interior and is open daily, 9:30 a.m. to 5 p.m. It is closed Christmas, Thanksgiving, and New Year's Day.

——————————— Roslyn ———————————

■

WILLIAM CULLEN BRYANT
Cedarmere

n 1845 American poet and newspaper editor William Cullen Bryant wrote to the critic Richard Henry Dana, "You cannot think what an interest I feel in (my own estate Roslyn). It is about as dear to me as one of my children — my heart yearned after it during the whole of my absence in Europe. I used to beguile the qualms of seasickness as I lay in my berth with thinking over my little plans for its improvement such as planting a fruit tree here and a shade tree there and clearing away the growth of shrubs about some fine young pear tree that has sprung up in a corner of my field."

By the time he purchased Cedarmere in 1844, Bryant was a well-known writer and critic. Born in 1794, he had written some of his best-known poetry, in which he celebrates nature, before he was 21 and had begun his professional life as a lawyer in Barrington, Massachusetts. He moved to New York City in 1825 and soon after began a lifetime association with the *New York Evening Post*. He purchased Cedarmere as his retreat away from the city but near enough to take advantage of the 19th-century artistic and literary world it offered—a world in which he played an important part. From 1844 to 1865 Bryant spent three-day weekends here, after which he

Cedarmere, purchased by Bryant in 1844.

spent longer periods. Cedarmere also served as a magnet for artists and writers seeking the writer's company until his death in 1878. (See William Cullen Bryant Homestead, page 104.)

Cedarmere today is an accurate reconstruction of the original residence. A fire in 1903 almost completely destroyed the stucco and frame colonial residence, but a Bryant descendant rebuilt the house soon after based on extant documents. The original house was built around 1789 by a Quaker farmer, Richard Kirk, who called the property Springback. Gothic Revival details were added much later by Bryant, who purchased the house from its third owner in 1844. The two-story house also has a three-dormer attic and porches embracing it on all sides. A central hall runs the length of the house with two rooms opening on it from either side. Bryant wrote much of his later romantic poetry in the library, described by a contemporary as a room of "generous dimensions." The fireplace on the south wall is adorned by old Dutch tiles with scriptural references. The tiles survived the 1903 fire.

Administered by the Nassau County Department of Recreation and Parks, the residence, currently not open to the public, is undergoing a thorough restoration. Cedarmere will reopen in 1993.

— Tarrytown —

■

WASHINGTON IRVING
Sunnyside

While Washington Irving is best remembered as America's first internationally successful author, Irving himself had a special passion for Sunnyside, transforming it from a small rural cottage to a unique residence expressing his personal tastes. In 1836, one year after purchasing the property, Irving wrote to his brother Peter, "I am living most cosily and delightfully in this dear, bright little house, which I have fitted up in my own humor. Everything goes on cheerily in my little household and I would not exchange the cottage for any chateau in Christendom."

Irving was born in New York City in 1783 and was named by his British-born parents after General George Washington. As a youth he developed a lasting fondness for the theater, music, art, travel, and society and briefly studied law in the offices of former Attorney General Josiah O. Hoffman. He became engaged to Hoffman's daughter, who died of tuberculosis before the marriage.

Under the pseudonym "Jonathan Oldstyle," Irving published nine essays in 1802–03 about the New York theater in his brother's newspaper *The Morning Chronicle*. After a two-year tour of Europe, he passed the New York State bar examination but continued writing under a pseudonym for *Salmagundi,* a humorous periodical published in 1807–08. The following year he published his satirical *History of New York,* which introduced the character Diedrich Knickerbocker and established the author's literary fame.

In 1815 he joined his brother in England hoping to revive the family's failing export business, but the firm's financial difficulties mounted with the Napoleonic Wars and it went bankrupt in 1818. Irving then turned his creative skills to writing for a living. In 1819–20 he published in serial form *The Sketch Book of Geoffrey Crayon, Gent,* which included his most famous stories, "Rip Van Winkle" and "The Legend of Sleepy Hollow."

The next years were spent abroad in diplomatic service during which a number of works grew out of his European experiences, including *Bracebridge Hall* in 1822, *Tales of a Traveller* in 1824, *The Life of Columbus* in 1828, and *The Alhambra* in 1832. Returning to the United States in 1832, and excited about seeing more of his own country, Irving joined an army expedition to the American West and wrote about his experiences in

A Tour of the Prairies in 1835. That same year he purchased the late 17th-century tenant farmer's house that was to become Sunnyside.

With the help of his friend George Harvey, a British-born painter, Irving remodelled the house, adding Dutch-stepped gables to the roof and Gothic and Romanesque architectural features to other parts. He turned down an opportunity to run for mayor of New York City and one political appointment in

Washington Irving's study, the center of the Sunnyside household. Here the author spent long hours writing, and it is where he usually received visitors.

order to remain at Sunnyside to continue his work on the property. In 1842 he finally did leave for four years to serve as U.S. minister to Spain.

At Sunnyside he wrote a number of works, including his five-volume biography of George Washington, published just before his death in 1859. Irving is buried at the Sleepy Hollow Cemetery in Tarrytown.

Today's visitor to Sunnyside sees it much as it appeared during the final years of the author's life: a book-lined study containing his writing desk and many personal possessions; a dining room and parlor, where Irving played the flute for his guests accompanied by his nieces Sarah and Catherine on the rosewood piano; a picture gallery off the parlor containing some original illustrations for Irving's work. The kitchen was advanced for its day, having a hot-water boiler and running water fed from the pond through a low-gravity system. The iron stove also was a modern convenience, replacing the open hearth in the 1850s.

The second floor of the house includes several bedrooms, each with its own personal character. Unusual arches in several of the rooms were designed by Irving. Irving's bedroom contains his Sheraton tester bed along with personal effects. The small bright room between Irving's bedroom and a guest bedroom might have been used by Irving's nephew and biographer, Pierre Munro Irving, who cared for his uncle during the last months of his life. This room originally had been used to store books and papers. The bedroom of the author's nieces includes an Irving family bed with handmade bobbin lace hangings, a chest of drawers, and sewing stands. A cast-iron bed in another guest room was probably made in one of the foundries along the Hudson.

Administered by Historic Hudson Valley, Sunnyside is open January and February weekends, 10 a.m. to 4 p.m.; April to October, daily except Tuesday, 10 a.m. to 5 p.m.; November, December, and March, daily, 10 a.m. to 4 p.m. It is closed Thanksgiving, Christmas, and New Year's Day.

——————————— Asheville ———————————

■

THOMAS WOLFE

Born in 1900, the youngest of eight children, Thomas Clayton Wolfe lived only 38 years. His parents' conflict and his mother's close attention greatly affected his adult life and character. Wolfe's family life began to deteriorate when Julia Wolfe, the author's mother, bought

Thomas Wolfe.

a boarding house in 1906. Her husband refused to become involved in the enterprise and remained at the family's former residence on Woodfin Street. Meanwhile, the boarding house became a primary residence for the children, who shuttled back and forth between the houses. The parents could not be reconciled, leaving the family in a perpetual state of turmoil, a turmoil reflected in Wolfe's own emotionally and physically turbulent life.

Upon graduating from the University of North Carolina in 1920, Thomas Wolfe entered Harvard Graduate School to study play writing under the celebrated Professor George P. Baker. He received his master of arts degree in 1922 and in 1924 accepted a teaching position with Washington Square College of New York University. When he had saved enough money, he embarked on the first of seven trips he would make to Europe in the next 12 years. It was in London in 1926 that he began his first novel, *Look Homeward, Angel,* published finally in 1929. The novel brought him fame and fortune and also the wrath of his family and the people of Asheville.

Wolfe was one of the most overly autobiographical of this country's major novelists. His own family and boyhood provided the material for many passages and characters in *Look Homeward, Angel* and its sequel, *Of Time and the River,* in 1935. The rambling Victorian boarding house run by his mother, known as Old Kentucky Home, served especially as the stage for the first novel. Called Dixieland in the book, the frame, gable roof house with its many porches provided the author with an abundance of diverse characters. After the book appeared, it was denounced publicly and privately in Asheville and was banned from the city's public libraries.

When he returned to the city in 1937, Wolfe found that most of the resentment against him had died, and the town as a whole was proud of its native son. Despite the warmth of

Early spring surrounding the boarding house once operated by Wolfe's mother. It is now called the Thomas Wolfe Memorial.

Asheville's welcome, he returned to New York and wrote in a letter, "Don't be surprised if some day you see a piece, 'You Can't Go Home Again.'" Indeed, this was one of the novels arranged by Wolfe's editor from material he left at his death.

In 1938 Wolfe made a long-desired journey to the West Coast, but while there he contracted a severe case of pneumonia. In hospital, a serious infection was detected. He was taken across country to the Johns Hopkins Hospital in Baltimore, where he underwent an operation that revealed tuberculosis of the brain. His death, two weeks before his 38th birthday, was a shock to his family, friends, and the literary world. He was buried in Riverside Cemetery in Asheville.

The restoration of the author's boyhood home, the boarding house run by his mother, has been based on the description of the boarding house and its inhabitants in *Look Homeward, Angel*. On entering the house, now called the Thomas Wolfe Memorial, the visitor steps backward a generation or two in time and into Wolfe's first novel. Here, many rooms, mementos, and furnishings are woven into the fact and fiction of his novel: the parlor where the boarders rocked within the protective circle of family portraits; the dining room where meals were served and the sun parlor where boarders sat in the evenings to listen to the novel's Helen Grant, daughter of the proprietress, play the piano and where they danced to a tune provided by a vintage phonograph. Mr. Grant's room includes the furniture suggested in the novel, his smoking stand, and walking canes. Adjoining this room is another displaying the office equipment and working tools from Mr. Grant's monument shop on the square. In the kitchen is a great iron stove, flat irons, and ironing board. Attached to the kitchen is the room of proprietress Eliza Grant, littered with her personal and business paraphernalia. A worn stairway leads to the sleeping porch and bedrooms above.

One room of the house is devoted to the author's personal effects. Furnishings from his New York apartment, including his typewriter and briefcase, an ancient brass lamp, the daybed purchased for his mother's use when she visited, and a battered suitcase reside here. Outside this room is a playhouse brought from the Woodfin Street home, the lone survivor of the author's birthplace two blocks away, just as the rambling old boarding house is the solitary reminder of this once tree-shaded residential district.

The Thomas Wolfe Memorial, administered by the North Carolina Division of Archives and History, is open April 1 to October 31, Monday to Saturday, 9 a.m. to 5 p.m., and Sunday, 1 to 5 p.m. From November 1 to March 31 it is open Tuesday to Saturday, 10 a.m. to 4 p.m., and Sunday, 1 to 4 p.m.

────────────── Flat Rock ──────────────

■

CARL SANDBURG
Connemara

When Carl Sandburg first came to the western North Carolina mountains in 1945 and stood on the porch of the main house of Connemara, he knew he had arrived at a place he could call home. He and his wife Lilian were enchanted with the beautiful environment and gentle climate. The farm had everything the family wanted, including ample pasture for the goats and seclusion for writing. Sandburg settled here with his family and spent the last 22 years of his life on this Flat Rock farm.

The house and farm had a long history. Christopher Gustavus Memminger of Charleston, S.C., had originally built the main residence around 1838 as his summer home. He later became the first secretary of the Confederate treasury and served in that capacity from 1861 to 1864. After his death, the property passed to the Gregg family and then to Captain Ellison Smyth, a textile tycoon. His heirs sold it to the Sandburgs in 1945, who moved to the 240-acre farm from Michigan with their three daughters and two grandchildren, a library of more than 10,000 volumes, all their personal belongings, and the Chikaming goat herd.

The Sandburg years at Connemara were productive. In 1948 Sandburg published his only novel, *Remembrance Rock,* which traced the American epic from Plymouth Rock to World War II. His autobiography, *Always the Young Strangers,* was published in 1953 and centered on his youth in Galesburg, Illinois (see Carl Sandburg Birthplace, page 50). These were followed by several volumes of history and poetry, including the *Complete Poems,* which won the Pulitzer Prize for Poetry in 1951.

Connemara, Carl Sandburg's idyllic farmhouse estate in the mountains.

Lilian Sandburg continued to breed and care for her prize-winning herd of goats, and she ran the farm business. Sandburg kept late hours. He usually began working, cigar in hand, in his cluttered upstairs workroom late in the evening and continued until the early hours of morning. Rising in late morning, he spent the afternoons reading and corresponding in a downstairs study or on the front porch overlooking the mountains.

Sandburg's study at Connemara, filled with the papers and books of an author's busy life.

Frequent guests, including the photographer Edward Steichen, Lilian Sandburg's brother, kept the household a vibrant and exciting place. With or without guests, the evening always meant a social gathering, with a family sing-along accompanied by Sandburg on his guitar or a reading from one of his current works. Sandburg's long and happy life here ended with his death in 1967.

At Lilian's death in 1977, the site became the property of the National Park Service.

The Sandburg home still displays the family's casual lifestyle. The dining and living rooms evoke the family's evening gatherings, while Sandburg's downstairs study, cluttered with filing boxes and books, attests to the author's varied interests. More than 10,000 books and thousands of papers and notes remain at the property today. Lilian Sandburg spent a good part of her time in the farm office. Her bedroom is on the first floor beyond the kitchen, while Sandburg's bedroom adjoined his top-floor office, where he did most of his writing. In the hallway is part of Sandburg's collection of stereographs, a reminder of the days he sold them as a college student. Over the front porch is a small room Sandburg named the Crow's Nest, where guests were lodged.

The Carl Sandburg Home National Historic Site is administered by the National Park Service, U.S. Department of the Interior. It is open daily, 9 a.m. to 5 p.m., except Christmas.

——————————— Columbus ———————————

■

JAMES THURBER

This unpretentious home of the 1870s is a fitting tribute to the creator of that shy and vulnerable character, Walter Mitty, a beleaguered "little man" who compensated for his timidity with a superactive fantasy life. Thurber himself was a shy and self-conscious man, handicapped

Pencil sketch of James Thurber by Milton Caniff.

by a blind left eye because of a childhood accident. This shyness perhaps led to his ability to be the special witness to the goings-on of his family at this house and others where his family lived in Columbus and to record these happenings in his writings, all characterized by wit and comic imagination.

Thurber, born in 1894, lived here between 1913 and 1917 while he attended college at Ohio State University. He lived with his parents, Charles and Mary Agnes, and his two brothers, William and Robert, and family episodes led to several of Thurber's tales, including "The Night the Bed Fell" and "The Night the Ghost Got In," both published in *The New Yorker* in 1933.

Thurber first developed as a writer at the *Columbus Dispatch*. Then, in 1926, a few months after selling a short story to the *The New Yorker*, he was hired as an editor for the then-new magazine. His friend and mentor on the magazine was the well-known stylist, E. B. White, with whom he collaborated in 1929 on *Is Sex Necessary?*, a parody of the popular self-help books of the 1920s.

White was responsible for the first appearance of Thurber's popular cartoons, which were to become a regular feature. Dorothy Parker once said of his drawings, "These are strange people that Mr. Thurber turned loose on us. . . . All of them have the outer semblance of unbaked cookies." Several collections of his drawings and writings were published, most of which appeared first in *The New Yorker*. He also wrote five books for children. His output was slowed only by his increasing loss of sight, which eventually made him resort to dictation. He died in 1961.

The James Thurber House is a restored modest Queen Anne home, typical of the late 19th century for a family of moderate means. The exterior restoration was based on a 1910 photograph of the house and any existing physical evidence that

The Thurber House, now host to an artist-in-residence program that attracts both writers and illustrators.

remained in the well-used dwelling, which had been both a music school and a boarding house. The interior restoration was based on the reminiscences of Thurber's brother Robert, who provided many details concerning the furnishings and possessions. Oak furniture, including Mission-style examples of the period, oiled pine flooring, beveled glass windows, and lace curtains all have been restored to the house. Thurber's room is furnished almost as sparsely as it had been some 75 years before, with a plain iron-frame bed, oak table and corner chair, and his Underwood-5 typewriter.

Today, Thurber House is an active writers center sponsoring a writers and artists residence program as well as readings and seminars. It is open every day except Christmas and New Year's Day, noon to 4 p.m.

—————————————— Dayton ——————————————

■

PAUL LAURENCE DUNBAR

Born in 1872, poet and author Paul Laurence Dunbar was the son of former slaves. His father, Joshua Dunbar, had escaped plantation bondage through the Underground Railroad to Canada but returned to the United States to serve in a Massachusetts volunteer regiment during the Civil War. After the conflict he chose Dayton, Ohio, as his home. Dunbar's mother, Matilda, freed from slavery after the Civil War, traveled to Ohio with her two small sons to be with her mother. There she met Joshua Dunbar, they married, and Paul was born.

Upon his parents' separation, Paul and his two stepbrothers were raised by their mother, who did washing and sewing to support her family. The boys took on odd jobs, such as lighting the streets of Dayton, to supplement the family's income. What their mother could not provide in material

Early portrait of Paul Laurence Dunbar.

wealth, she provided in inspiration, especially to her youngest son, giving Paul a treasure trove of stories and folklore and a love of song and poetry.

Dunbar wrote his first poem at the age of six and later recited publicly for the first time at age 12. At Dayton's Central

House purchased by the poet when he returned to his birth
city in 1903.

High School, he was the only African American, but he found
here support and acceptance. He was named to the prestigious
Philomathean Literary Society and later became its president.
He also edited the school newspaper. School officials, discov-
ering his writing talent, encouraged him to pursue a literary
career. To support himself after graduation, he took a job as
an elevator boy but continued to write, producing poems for
the Chicago newspaper syndicate and various national African
American newspapers. His first book of poetry, *Oak and Ivy*,
published in 1893, brought him some praise and attention but

not financial independence. A break in his career came when he met H. A. Tobey, superintendent of the Toledo State Hospital. Tobey became his friend and benefactor and, together with Toledo attorney Charles Thatcher, provided resources to publish Dunbar's second book, *Majors and Minors,* which came to the attention of literary critic William Dean Howells. The critic's favorable review in *Harper's Weekly* made Dunbar a national literary figure. Dodd, Mead and Company combined the poet's two collections of poems into one title, *Lyrics of a Lowly Life,* with an introduction by Howells. Dunbar received wide acclaim for this work, published in 1896, and was invited to tour England.

On his return from England he married Alice Ruth Moore and settled in Washington, D.C., where he took a position with the Library of Congress. Because of his growing acclaim, he soon left the library to devote himself full time to writing and giving recitals of his work. In 1898 he published his first novel, *The Uncalled,* and a volume of short stories, *Folks from Dixie.* Other stories and novels, even musicals and operettas, as well as hundreds of poems, many the dialect poetry that was so popular, were to follow.

Dunbar wrote about the black experience in the United States, and he was well known for his use of dialect. In addition to listening to the language of former slaves he had met through his mother, he had studied the dialect techniques of Joel Chandler Harris and James Whitcomb Riley in their works. He also was an effective and strong national voice for equality and justice for African Americans, speaking and writing frequently on civil rights. His poem, "We Wear the Mask," eloquently states some of his concerns.

The poet and author returned to Dayton in 1903. Suffering from tuberculosis, he was also disheartened by a separation from his wife. Purchasing this solid brick house at 219 Summit Street, he lived here with his mother until his death in 1906. Matilda Dunbar remained in the house until her own death in 1934, preserving her son's books and manuscripts and his "loafing holt"—his study. At her death, the state of Ohio purchased the property, turning it over to the Ohio Historical Society, which administers it as a state memorial.

The Paul Laurence Dunbar House has been restored to its turn-of-the-century elegance. Among the objects on view are the desk and typewriter the poet used to compose much of his poetry, the ceremonial sword presented him by President Theodore Roosevelt, and the bicycle given him by Wilbur and Orville Wright, with whom he had attended school.

The property is open Memorial Day to Labor Day, Wednesday to Saturday, 9:30 a.m. to 5 p.m., and on Sunday, noon to 5 p.m. From September to October it is open Saturday, 9:30 a.m. to 5 p.m., and Sunday, noon to 5 p.m.

—————————————— Lucas ——————————————

■

LOUIS BROMFIELD
Malabar Farm

During the 1920s and 1930s, Louis Bromfield was one of the most popular novelists in the United States. *The Green Bay Tree*, published in 1925, launched his literary career. During his lifetime he wrote 33 books and numerous screenplays. His novels such as *The Rains Came, Night in Bombay, Mrs. Parkington*, and *Early Autumn,* for which he won a Pulitzer Prize, were published in more than 15 languages.

Bromfield was born in Mansfield, not far from Malabar Farm, in 1896. After graduating from high school, he studied journalism and agriculture in college but left his studies to drive an ambulance with the French army during World War I. After the war, he returned to the United States where he renewed his interest both in writing and agriculture. In 1921 he married Mary Appleton Wood and began an active writing career. With the Pulitzer Prize money from *Early Autumn* in his pocket in 1927, he returned to France with his wife and daughter. The visit lasted 12 years until Bromfield, with his wife and three daughters, decided to return to Ohio at the start of World War II.

In 1939 he purchased four farms southeast of Mansfield to create the sort of farm he had planned for years. He named it Malabar Farm after the Malabar Coast of India, the setting of his novel *The Rains Came*. The site originally included 640

Bromfield's sprawling house, one of several structures on view at Malabar Farm.

acres of woods, pasture, farmland, springs, and streams. Bromfield's farming practices were effective and progressive. Through a coordinated program of soil, water, forest, and wildlife conservation, he restored unproductive and eroded acreage to fertility. Large quantities of forage and pasture were produced, the

Louis Bromfield.

soil was renewed, and drainage improved. Contour plowing arrested erosion. He developed a planned forestry program and replaced traditional wire fencing with hedges of multiflora rose.

Throughout the 1940s he developed Malabar Farm as an agricultural showplace, attracting people from all over the world. It was also a haven for Hollywood favorites such as Humphrey Bogart, James Cagney, and Kay Francis. Bogart and Lauren Bacall were married there. During the 1950s the farm ran into financial troubles, in part because of the author's generous support of various worldwide conservation and wildlife projects. In 1956 Bromfield died in Columbus, Ohio, and Malabar passed to his daughters. Unable to maintain the farm, they turned it over to a nonprofit conservation foundation that their father had helped establish. Finally, in 1972 it was given to the state of Ohio, which had pledged to continue operating the site as a working farm, preserving its beauty and ecological balance.

The residence of the family, known as the Big House, was built with the help of architect Louis Lamoreaux using a small existing farmhouse as a base. The sprawling 32-room home is a blend of colonial and Victorian architectural styles and was furnished with much of the furniture the family had acquired in France, including original paintings and antiques collected over the years. Today, the house is just as Bromfield left it. Other farm structures are the smokehouse, silo, corn crib, dairy barn, chicken house, greenhouse, and tool shed.

Malabar Farm is part of Malabar Farm State Park, one of the state's most unusual parks and a memorial to this popular American author. In addition to the farm, other features include a youth hostel; the house where Bromfield lived while the Big House was being constructed; the Old Bailey Farm, one of the four original farms on the property; and the cemetery where the author, his wife, sister, and parents are interred.

The site is open April 1 to October 31 every day, 10 a.m. to 5 p.m., and from November 1 to March 31, every day except Monday, 11 a.m. to 5 p.m.

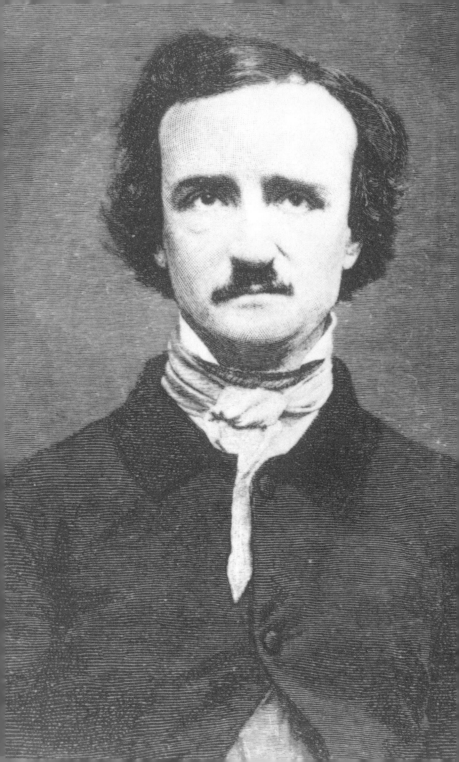

──────────────── Philadelphia ────────────────

■

EDGAR ALLAN POE

Noted poet and author of the macabre and the melancholy, Edgar Allan Poe moved to Philadelphia from New York City with his wife and cousin, Virginia, and his mother-in-law and aunt, Maria Clemm. The small family was to remain in Philadelphia renting several residences between 1837 and 1844 when Poe and Virginia returned to New York City.

The itinerant writer found better success in Philadelphia than he had in New York. Here he wrote some of his greatest short stories, including "The Gold Bug," "The Fall of the House of Usher," "The Tell-Tale Heart," and "The Murders in the Rue Morgue." Philadelphia rivaled New York in its literary output and welcomed a known writer who could contribute to its many magazines. In addition, Poe did not suffer from a poor reputation for drinking and had not alienated any part of the literary establishment as he had tended to do in New York.

Exactly how long Poe lived in the small brick house now connected to 530 North Seventh Street is not known. Apparently, he, Virginia, and Mrs. Clemm moved there sometime between fall 1842 and June 1843 and left April 1844. Like all of Poe's homes, this one was rented. It may or may not have been furnished when the family and their cat Caterina moved in. Whatever furniture they used or purchased has disappeared without a trace. Because of the lack of information about how the house might have been furnished (in fact, only a small number of objects, including two hooks, a cane, and a trunk,

Poet and author of the macabre, Edgar Allan Poe.

One of Edgar Allan Poe's rented residences in Philadelphia, where he lived with his young wife and her mother, Maria Clemm.

can actually be traced to Poe's ownership in his lifetime), the house stands empty of material. Only the spirit of Poe's works remains.

The importance of this house lies in its location and its connection to the author. During the six years that Poe lived in Philadelphia, he attained his greatest successes as an editor and critic, working for literary magazines and even endeavoring to establish his own journal. It was also in Philadelphia that Virginia's health began to deteriorate. Of Poe's several homes in this city, only this one survives, serving as a tangible link with Poe and his days of greatness in Philadelphia. (See Edgar Allan Poe Home, page 78, and Edgar Allan Poe Cottage, page 143.)

The survival of the house is due to the efforts of the late Colonel Richard Gimbel, a Poe scholar and collector. Gimbel purchased the site through a foundation in 1933 and, thereafter, maintained it as a museum. In 1980 the property was transferred to the National Park Service of the U.S. Department of the Interior. The site, consisting of the house and a visitor center, was opened in August of that year as the Edgar Allan Poe National Historic Site.

It is open Tuesday to Saturday, 9 a.m. to 5 p.m., and is closed Thanksgiving, Christmas, and New Year's Day.

TEXAS

■

O. HENRY

William Sydney Porter, otherwise known as O. Henry, was born at Worth Place, a plantation near Greensboro, North Carolina, in 1862. After his mother's death in 1865, he, his physician father, and brother moved into Greensboro to live with his grandmother and maiden aunt Evalina Porter, who ran a private school in the home. Porter attended this school until he was 15 and then attended public high school. At 17 he became an apprentice in his uncle's drugstore and after four years became a licensed pharmacist.

In 1882 Porter developed a bad cough and traveled to Texas to live and rest at a ranch run by the son of his friend and physician James K. Hall. Once his health had improved, he remained at the ranch, spending the next two years as an occasional cook and handyman. In 1884 Porter move in with friends in Austin with whom he stayed for three years, working at various jobs and enjoying the city's social life. Here he met Athol Estes and in 1887 eloped with her.

For the next four years Porter was employed as a draftsman in the city's land office, during which time the couple had a son who lived only a few hours. A daughter, Margaret Worth Porter, followed in 1889.

Porter lost his political appointment with the land office in 1891 with the election of a new governor. Forced to find work, he became a teller at the First National Bank of Austin. It is

William Sydney Porter, who sold his short stories under the pseudonym O. Henry while serving a prison sentence.

during this period that the family moved into this cottage on Fourth Street in 1893. Their three years here were difficult ones: Athol's health began to fail and Porter became increasingly unhappy with his bank position. Hoping to find a new avenue, Porter founded a journal in 1894 called *The Rolling Stone,* in which he published his own short stories. He gave up the publication the next year just a few months after losing his job at the bank because of suspicious shortages in his accounting books. He moved to Houston to take a job as a columnist for the *Houston Post,* but he was indicted eight months later for embezzlement. Sending his wife and daughter to Austin, he fled the country from New Orleans where he took a banana boat to Honduras.

Cottage where Porter lived with his wife and daughter. The author's years here were particularly difficult ones.

In exile he began to make plans to have his family join him, but at the urging of his mother-in-law, he returned to Austin to see Athol whose health had rapidly deteriorated. For a short time she rallied, but tuberculosis gained the upper hand and she died in 1897.

While awaiting his trial in the six months following his wife's death, Porter sold his first short story to a national publication. At his three-day trial, during which Porter was silent throughout, he was found guilty and sentenced to five years in a Ohio penitentiary. Before his release in 1901 he had served as a pharmacist in the prison hospital and had perfected his writing craft, selling his short stories under the pseudonym O. Henry. After prison, he moved to New York City where, over the next eight years until his death in 1910, he published 381 stories and became America's favorite short-story writer. (See O. Henry House, below.)

Administered by Austin's Cultural Affairs Division, the O. Henry Museum at 409 East Fifth Street is open Wednesday to Sunday, noon to 5 p.m.

—————————————— San Antonio ——————————————

■

O. HENRY

In 1894 William Sydney Porter, who later was to take the pseudonym O. Henry, founded his own satirical weekly journal and called it *The Rolling Stone*. Porter hoped the success of the newspaper, in which he published his own short stories, would allow him to leave a teller position with a bank in Austin (see O. Henry Museum, page 186).

To improve the newspaper's circulation, Porter established a San Antonio edition as well as an Austin edition, working out of this stucco house, then on South Presa Street. Porter made frequent visits here conferring with the newspaper's

manager and editor, Henry Ryder Taylor. The house originally
had been built in 1855 by John Kush, a pioneer stonemason,
as an investment. A variety of tenants followed. Porter's visits
and contact with the building were sufficient to endear the site
to the author's admirers, who had the small house dismantled
in 1960 and reassembled on the grounds of the Lone Star
Brewing Company. The move saved the building from certain
demolition.

The O. Henry House, where mementos and personal possessions related to Porter are exhibited, is part of a complex
of sites pertinent to Texas history administered by the Lone
Star Brewery. It is open daily 9:30 a.m. to 5 p.m.

House that William Sydney Porter often visited while establishing
his satirical journal. It was after this period that Porter assumed
the nom de plume O. Henry.

———————————— Richmond ————————————

■

ELLEN GLASGOW

Novelist Ellen Glasgow was born in 1874 in Richmond, the eighth of 11 children, to Francis Thomas Glasgow, a strict Scottish Presbyterian, and Anne Jane Gholson Glasgow, a descendant of an aristocratic Tidewater Virginia family. Attracted to being alone, she suffered an unhappy childhood beset with various illnesses and an obsession with fear.

Glasgow's formal education was quite limited. She attended school, in her own words, "a few months each year, until my health grew frail again and my nervous headaches returned." Her sister's husband, George Walter McCormack, exercised a vital

Novelist Ellen Glasgow, whose works studied the changing roles of women in the South.

influence over the young Ellen Glasgow's academic and intellectual development by guiding her reading. She became a radical thinker for her day, emphasizing in her works a changing social order that included the important roles of the middle class and particularly women. Her interest in socialism led her to read works of the Fabians, in particular, George Bernard Shaw.

At 24 Glasgow published her first novel, *The Descendant,* under a pseudonym. With the exception of *Life and Gabriella,* published in 1916, all of her works were written in her upstairs study of this Greek Revival house in Richmond. Several earned her literary distinctions, including *In This Our Life,* published in 1941 and for which she received the Pulitzer Prize.

Glasgow's interests led to travels all over the world during which she became acquainted with many great literary figures. She also worked among the poor and homeless. She died in 1945 following a long illness.

Built in 1841, the stuccoed Greek Revival house at One West Main Street is characteristic of buildings of the 1830s and 1840s in Richmond. Ellen Glasgow was 13 when her father purchased it and moved his family here. The house would remain her home for the rest of her life.

The northwest room on the second floor, the novelist's study, includes the wallpaper she imported from England. The southeast room is her bedroom diagonally across the hall. The only original furnishings in the house are a crystal chandelier in the front drawing room, removed in 1887 and reinstalled in 1947, and a large mirror over the fireplace. A wing was added in 1917, eliminating the porch extensions in the rear.

In 1982 a law firm purchased and occupied the residence. Since 1986 the house has been the residence of the John W. Pearsall III family, with the firm occupying the English basement. While it is not open to the public, the owner occasionally will show the house to interested parties.

Glasgow's house, now a private residence with offices installed in the basement.

--------- Hillsboro ---------

■

PEARL S. BUCK

Pearl S. Buck was born in this board-and-batten house but lived here but a few months. Built about 1880 by the author's Dutch-descended great grandfather, Mynheer Johann Stulting, the Pearl S. Buck Birthplace also is known locally as the Stulting Place.

Buck's parents were missionaries home on furlough when she was born in 1892. After only four months, her parents returned with her to China where the author learned to speak Chinese before she had learned English.

For a short time Buck attended a Chinese school, but most of her early education was provided by her mother. At 17 she returned to America to attend the Randolph-Macon College for Women. After graduating, she went back to China and there met her husband, John Lossing Buck, a missionary specializing in advising Chinese farmers on agricultural matters. While a professor at Nanking University where she taught English literature, Buck published her first work, an essay in *Atlantic Monthly.* This was followed by articles and stories in several American and Chinese periodicals.

In 1930 *East Wind: West Wind* became her first novel of the Orient, followed in 1931 by *The Good Earth,* a remarkable study of Chinese peasant life and her best-known work, which earned her the Pulitzer Prize. In the years that followed she wrote other works, including biographies of her parents, *The Exile* and *Fighting Angel,* both of which appeared in 1936. In 1938 she received the Nobel Prize for Literature, making her one of two

Pearl S. Buck.

authors to receive both the Pulitzer and Nobel prizes, the other being John Steinbeck. Pearl Buck died in Vermont in 1973.

In *The Exile* the novelist gives some details about building the family home: "There, at the edge of the settlement, they built it. A goodly 12-room house of wood, with smooth floors and plastered and papered walls, a city house. The wood they took from their own land. It took a long time to build, more than two years."

Today, the birthplace is very much the same as when it was built. It is a vernacular structure showing a mix of Greek Revival, Italianate, and Carpenter Gothic elements. The three-window bay most likely was added later, together with two rooms at the back. The floors, woodwork, stairs, and most of the other details are just as they came from the hands of the Stulting builders.

Many of the furnishings are original to the family, including two cabinets, or "presses," as they were called, in the front parlor; the "Sunburst" quilt on the four-poster bed in the birth room; a bench in the kitchen; the family's organ; and shelves filled with books.

The Pearl S. Buck Birthplace is administered by the Pearl S. Buck Birthplace Foundation and is open Monday to Saturday, 9 a.m. to 5 p.m., and on Sunday, 1 to 5 p.m.

Pearl S. Buck Birthplace, an eclectic mix of several architectural styles built by the author's great grandfather.

WISCONSIN

─────────── West Salem ───────────

■

HAMLIN GARLAND

Hamlin Garland was born in 1860 in a log cabin. The hardships of pioneer life were always the predominant theme of Garland's books, and his life on the Wisconsin frontier had the deepest influence on his writings. In his autobiography he wrote, "My Wisconsin birthplace has always been a source of deep satisfaction to me."

Set in an area around La Crosse near the town of West Salem,

House built by Garland for his parents as a log cabin in a wooded area. Time has contributed to the house's changes, although the basic form of the original homestead is the same.

his collections of stories, including *Main Traveled Roads,* published in 1881, and *Prairie Folks,* published in 1893, and novels such as *Rose of Dutcher's Coolly,* published in 1895, give a vivid description of the hardships of pioneer life as well as the social practices of rural Wisconsin. This passage from *Main Traveled Roads* best expresses the theme of his works: "The lives of these farmers are hard, parched by the sun and tanned by the wind. No beauty, no music, no art, no joy, just a dull and hopeless round of toil."

His "Middle Border" series is crowded with autobiographical material, rich with portraits taken from Wisconsin's history. These include *A Son of the Middle Border* of 1917 and *A Daughter of the Middle Border* of 1921.

When he was older, Garland's family moved to Iowa, where he graduated from Cedar Valley Seminary in Osage in 1881. When his family moved farther west to homestead the Dakota Territory, he wandered about taking odd jobs. In 1884 he settled in Boston to continue his schooling. He married Zulime Taft, sister of a Chicago sculptor, in 1899 and had two daughters.

He remained close to his parents throughout his life, eventually purchasing for them this cabin and four acres in West Salem in 1893 as a homestead. He spent a considerable amount of time here — four to five months each year after his marriage — writing and raising his family. The house was partially destroyed by fire in 1912 but was rebuilt.

Garland spent the last 10 years of his life in Southern California near his daughter. He died in 1940.

In 1973 the U.S. Department of the Interior designated the house a National Historic Landmark. It was purchased by the West Salem Historical Society that same year, and restoration began in 1975. Several pieces of original Garland furniture are on display as well as books, paintings, and other objects.

The Hamlin Garland Homestead is open Memorial Day to Labor Day, Monday to Saturday, 1 to 5 p.m.

Hamlin Garland in the homestead's study.

PHOTOGRAPHIC CREDITS

London: California State Park System, Jack London Collection

Muir: John Muir National Historic Site

O'Neill: portrait, Library of Congress; house, National Park Service

Stevenson: portrait, Library of Congress

Stowe: The Stowe-Day Foundation

Twain: Mark Twain Memorial

Webster: portrait, Metropolitan Museum of Art

Hemingway: portrait, Hemingway Society, John F. Kennedy Library; house and studio, Ernest Hemingway Home and Museum

Harris: Joel Chandler Harris Association

Lanier: Middle Georgia Historical Society

Sandburg: portrait, Illinois State Historical Library; birthplace, Illinois Historic Preservation Agency

Lindsay: Vachel Lindsay Association, Herbert Georg Studio

Riley: portrait, Library of Congress; birthplace, © 1991 Phil Hollenbaugh; home, Ed. Lacey, Jr., Photography

Stratton-Porter: Gene Stratton-Porter State Historic Site

Robinson: portrait, Pirie MacDonald, New York

Longfellow: Portland, Maine Historical Society; Cambridge, National Park Service

Jewett: Society for the Preservation of New England Antiquities

Poe: portrait, Edgar Allan Poe National Historic Site; Baltimore, Jeff Jerome, Edgar Allan Poe House; Bronx, Bronx County Historical Society; Philadelphia, Russell P. Smith, National Park Service

Whittier: portrait, Library of Congress

Dickinson: Amherst College

Prescott: portrait, Massachusetts Historical Society; house, National Society of the Colonial Dames of America

Alcott: house, Nancy Hill-Joroff

Emerson: house, © 1991 Bonnie McGrath

Thoreau: portrait, Thoreau Lyceum; cabin at the lyceum, Bonnie McGrath; cabin in the woods, John Suiter

Melville: portrait, Berkshire Athenaeum, Herman Melville Memorial Room

Lardner: portrait, Library of Congress

Faulkner: University of Mississippi; house and work area, Robert Jordan

Cather: Nebraska State Historical Society

Aldrich: house, Strawbery Banke

Whitman: portrait, National Portrait Gallery, Smithsonian Institution

Roosevelt: portrait, Harvard College Library, Theodore Roosevelt Collection; house, National Park Service

Bryant: Nassau County Museum

Thurber: Thurber House

Dunbar: Ohio Historical Society

Bromfield: portrait, Ohio State University; house, Tom Root

O. Henry: portrait and Austin house, Austin Public Library

Glasgow: portrait, Virginia State Library and Archives; house, Richmond Newspapers

Buck: portrait, Library of Congress

Garland: West Salem Historical Society

AMERICAN AUTHORS
AND THEIR HOMES

Louisa May Alcott

Orchard House
399 Lexington Road
Concord, MA 01742
(508) 369-4118

Thomas Bailey Aldrich

Thomas Bailey Aldrich
    Memorial
Strawbery Banke
P.O. Box 300
Portsmouth, NH 03801
(603) 436-1100

Louis Bromfield

Malabar Farm
Malabar Farm State Park
4050 Bromfield Road
Lucas, OH 44843
(419) 892-2784

William Cullen Bryant

William Cullen Bryant
    Homestead
Route 112
Cummington, MA 01026
(413) 634-2244

Cedarmere
1 Museum Drive
Roslyn, NY 11576
(516) 484-9338

Pearl S. Buck

Pearl S. Buck Birthplace
U.S. Highway 219 (Box 126)
Hillsboro, WV 24946
(304) 653-4430

Willa Cather

Willa Cather Childhood Home
Willa Cather Historical Center
338 North Webster Street
Red Cloud, NE 68970
(402) 746-3285

Emily Dickinson

Emily Dickinson Homestead
280 Main Street
Amherst, MA 01002
(413) 542-8161

Paul Laurence Dunbar

Paul Laurence Dunbar House
219 North Summit Street
Dayton, OH 45407
(513) 224-7061

Ralph Waldo Emerson

Ralph Waldo Emerson House
28 Cambridge Turnpike
Concord, MA 01742
(508) 263-0832

William Faulkner

Rowan Oak
Old Taylor Road
Oxford, MS 38655
(601) 234-4655

Robert Frost

Robert Frost Farm
On State Route 28
Derry, NH 03038
(603) 432-3091

Hamlin Garland

Hamlin Garland Homestead
357 Garland Street
West Salem, WI 54669
(608) 786-1399

Ellen Glasgow

Ellen Glasgow House
One Main Street
Richmond, VA 23220
(804) 644-5491

Joel Chandler Harris

The Wren's Nest
1050 Gordon Street, S.W.
Atlanta, GA 30310
(404) 753-7735

Nathaniel Hawthorne

Nathaniel Hawthorne
   Birthplace
55 Turner Street
Salem, MA 01970-5698
(508) 744-0991

Ernest Hemingway

Ernest Hemingway Home and
   Museum
907 Whitehead Street
Key West, FL 33040
(305) 294-1575

O. Henry

O. Henry Museum
409 East Fifth Street
Austin, TX 78701
(512) 472-1903

O. Henry House
600 Lone Star Boulevard
San Antonio, TX 78204
(512) 226-8301

Washington Irving

Sunnyside
Historic Hudson Valley
150 White Plains Road
Tarrytown, NY 10591
(914) 591-8763

Sarah Orne Jewett

Sarah Orne Jewett House
5 Portland Street
South Berwick, ME 03908
(207) 384-5269

Sidney Lanier

Sidney Lanier Birthplace
935 High Street
Macon, GA 31201
(912) 743-3851

Ring Lardner

Ring Lardner Home
519 Bond Street
Niles, MI 49120

Sinclair Lewis

Sinclair Lewis Boyhood Home
Sinclair Lewis Avenue
Sauk Centre, MN 56378
(612) 352-6119

Vachel Lindsay

Vachel Lindsay Home
603 South Fifth Street
Springfield, IL 62703
(217) 528-9254 or
(217) 785-7960

Jack London

Jack London State Historic
Park
2400 London Ranch Road
Glen Ellen, CA 95442
(703) 938-5216

Henry Wadsworth Longfellow

Wadsworth-Longfellow House
485 Congress Street
Portland, ME 04101
(207) 772-1807

Longfellow Home National
Historic Site
105 Brattle Street
Cambridge, MA 02138
(617) 876-4491

Herman Melville

Arrowhead
780 Holmes Road
Pittsfield, MA 01201
(413) 442-1793

Christopher Morley

Knothole
Christopher Morley Park
Searington Road
North Hills, NY 11576
(516) 420-5290

John Muir

John Muir National Historic
Site
4202 Alhambra Avenue
Martinez, CA 94553
(415) 228-8860

Eugene O'Neill

Tao House
Eugene O'Neill National
Historic Site
P.O. Box 280
Danville, CA 94526
(415) 838-0249

Edgar Allan Poe

Edgar Allan Poe Home
203 North Amity Street
Baltimore, MD 21222
(301) 396-7932

Edgar Allan Poe Cottage
Grand Concourse and East
Kingsbridge Road
Bronx, NY 10467
(212) 881-8900

Edgar Allan Poe National
  Historic Site
532 North Seventh Street
Philadelphia, PA 19123
(215) 597-8780

William Hickling Prescott

William H. Prescott House
55 Beacon Street
Boston, MA 02108
(617) 742-3190

Marjorie Kinnan Rawlings

Rawlings State Historic Site
State Route 3 (Box 92)
Cross Creek, FL 32640
(904) 466-3672

James Whitcomb Riley

James Whitcomb Riley
  Birthplace
250 West Main Street
Greenfield, IN 46140
(317) 462-8539

James Whitcomb Riley Home
528 Lockerbie Street
Indianapolis, IN 46202
(317) 631-5885

Edwin Arlington Robinson

Edwin Arlington Robinson
  Home
67 Lincoln Avenue
Gardiner, ME 04345
(207) 582-3717

Theodore Roosevelt

Theodore Roosevelt Birthplace
28 East 20th Street
New York, NY 10003
(212) 260-1616

Sagamore Hill National
  Historic Site
Cove Neck Road (Box 304)
Oyster Bay, NY 11771
(516) 922-4447

Carl Sandburg

Carl Sandburg Birthplace
331 East Third Street
Galesburg, IL 61401
(309) 342-2361

Carl Sandburg Home National
  Historic Site
1928 Little River Road
Flat Rock, NC 28731
(704) 693-4178

Robert Louis Stevenson

Stevenson House
530 Houston Street
Monterey, CA 93940
(408) 649-7118

Harriet Beecher Stowe

Harriet Beecher Stowe House
Stowe-Day Foundation
77 Forest Street
Hartford, CT 06105
(203) 522-9258

Gene Stratton-Porter

Cabin in Wildflower Woods
Gene Stratton-Porter State
  Historic Site
Box 639
Rome City, IN 46784
(317) 232-1637

Henry David Thoreau

Cabin at Walden Pond
Walden Pond State
  Reservation
915 Walden Street
Concord, MA 01742
(508) 369-3264

Cabin at Walden Pond
Thoreau Lyceum
156 Belknap Street
Concord, MA 01742
(617) 369-5912

James Thurber

The Thurber House
77 Jefferson Avenue
Columbus, OH 43215
(614) 464-1032

Mark Twain

Mark Twain Memorial
351 Farmington Avenue
Hartford, CT 06105
(203) 525-9317

Noah Webster

Noah Webster Birthplace
227 South Main Street
West Hartford, CT 06107
(203) 521-5362

Edith Wharton

The Mount
Plunkett Street (P.O. Box 974)
Lenox, MA 01240
(413) 637-1899

Walt Whitman

Walt Whitman House
330 Mickle Street
Camden, NJ 08103
(609) 726-1191 or
(609) 964-5383

Walt Whitman House
  (birthplace)
246 Old Walt Whitman Road
Huntington, NY 11746
(516) 427-5240

John Greenleaf Whittier

John Greenleaf Whittier Home
86 Friend Street
Amesbury, MA 01913
(508) 388-1337

Thomas Wolfe

Thomas Wolfe Memorial
48 Spruce Street
Asheville, NC 28807
(704) 253-8304

INDEX TO AUTHORS

Alcott, Louisa May, 95

Aldrich, Thomas Bailey, 137

Bromfield, Louis, 178

Bryant, William Cullen, 104, 157

Buck, Pearl S., 195

Cather, Willa, 130

Clemens, Samuel. *See* Twain, Mark

Dickinson, Emily, 84

Dunbar, Paul, 174

Emerson, Ralph Waldo, 97

Faulkner, William, 127

Frost, Robert, 133

Garland, Hamlin, 197

Glasgow, Ellen, 191

Harris, Joel Chandler, 45

Hawthorne, Nathaniel, 115

Hemingway, Ernest, 39

Henry, O., 186, 189

Irving, Washington, 159

Jewett, Sarah Orne, 73

Lanier, Sidney, 47

Lardner, Ring, 119

Lewis, Sinclair, 123

Lindsay, Vachel, 55

London, Jack, 10

Longfellow, Henry Wadsworth, 69, 91

Melville, Herman, 110

Morley, Christopher, 150

Muir, John, 14

O'Neill, Eugene, 18

Poe, Edgar Allan, 78, 143, 183

Porter, William Sydney. *See* Henry, O.

Prescott, William Hickling, 87

Rawlings, Marjorie Kinnan, 36

Riley, James Whitcomb, 59, 61

Robinson, Edwin Arlington, 67

Roosevelt, Theodore, 148, 153

Sandburg, Carl, 50, 167

Stevenson, Robert Louis, 21

Stowe, Harriet Beecher, 24

Stratton-Porter, Gene, 63

Thoreau, Henry David, 101

Thurber, James, 171

Twain, Mark, 29

Webster, Noah, 33

Wharton, Edith, 107

Whitman, Walt, 141, 145

Whittier, John Greenleaf, 81

Wolfe, Thomas, 163

ABOUT THE AUTHOR

Irvin Haas has spent his long life devoted to books and book publishing. His interest in fine limited editions and fine prints began in his teen years. He has written several books, including *A Treasury of Great Prints, America's Historic Houses and Restorations*, and *America's Historic Inns and Taverns*. He was prints editor of *Art News* for 12 years. *Historic Homes of American Authors* is the ninth book he has written on America's historic sites.